ZIGGURAT

Also by Ivan Southall

Ziggurat

ivan southall

Viking
Penguin Books Australia Ltd
487 Maroondah Highway, PO Box 257
Ringwood, Victoria 3134, Australia
Penguin Books Ltd
Harmondsworth, Middlesex, England
Viking Penguin, A Division of Penguin Books USA Inc.
375 Hudson Street, New York, New York 10014, USA
Penguin Books Canada Limited
10 Alcorn Avenue, Toronto, Ontario, Canada M4V 3B2
Penguin Books (N.Z.) Ltd
Cnr Rosedale and Airborne Roads, Albany, Auckland, New Zealand

First published by Penguin Books Australia, 1997
1 3 5 7 9 10 8 6 4 2
Copyright © Ivan Southall, 1997

Typeset in 10.5/17 Sabon by Post Typesetters
Made and printed in Australia by Australian Print Group,
Maryborough, Victoria

Cover and text design by Ruth Grüner
Cover photography by Denise Nestor

National Library of Australia
Cataloguing-in-Publication data:

Southall, Ivan, 1921–.
Ziggurat.

ISBN 0 670 87770 0.

I. Title.

A823.3

Quotation from the hymn 'Day is dying in the west' by Mary A.
Lathbury (American, 1841–1913) on p197 has been taken from
the *Methodist Hymn Book* (Australian Edition of 1904).

DEDICATION

My dog, hard against my desk, might well be saying
to me: 'Taki is the name, sir, but Sam will do.'

DEFINITION

Ziggurat: a structure of clay, historically of seven levels, that reaches for the heavens and invites the gods to come down.

KNUT MANNERHEIM CANUTE, aged seventeen, disappears from his home after midnight on July 4, leaving no evidence to confirm that he went by compulsion or of his own accord. He awakens to another mode of existence, another face of time, and is severely tested through periods of high challenge in a disintegrating world, a world that may be a mirror image of his own – or in parallel – or alien.

By degrees he comes to understand who he is, what he is, and where he is. Finally, he knows why this journey sought him out, picked him up, and carried him along.

CONTENTS

PART ONE
THE UNIVERSE
IS A HALL OF
MIRRORS

THE FAIRYTALES OF
KNUT AND NANETTE

Knut and Nanette reflect upon
the perils of love.

Suburbia. July. A distance south of the Tropic of Capricorn. A dozen or two degrees below the comfort zone. This was a mere five days following the unexpected return from Honolulu of Knut's father, the architect, known in his profession as the great man.

Winter.

The streets are classically tree-lined. A few are pleasantly clothed with evergreens in the antipodean manner. But most are bare-limbed, originating in the nineteenth century among immigrants of innocent mind tending their old-world seedlings in safe places on deck. Of a consequence, a century or more later, no guilty passer-by had anywhere to hide his person.

Monday. Which made it the evening of July 3.

Two incredibly long hours might have passed since sunset, but in no fair-minded society could a clean-cut male like Knut, aged seventeen, be accused of questionable conduct by hastening through the evening with a female counterpart, Nanette, aged sixteen, attached by the hand. Each young person being of good character by any measure, acknowledging the limitations of the human condition. Well, conduct not *seriously* questionable except by house masters of an earlier age, hospital matrons of a matching vintage and elderly ladies and gentlemen at second-floor levels peering through opera glasses. And by clear-eyed parents with appreciations of the jack-booted laws of inheritance.

Nevertheless, in the case of each young person, required home studies had been attended to, superficially, and out on the street it was hardly raining at all and barely seven-thirty. Yet the lad's soft shoes went padding from slab to slab with atypical anxiety and stealth – rendered clearly visible by brilliant street lighting and these trees without leaves.

Knut (pronounced Nut, we are told) padding along with occasional flares of panic; toes bruising on the ridges between slabs displaced by the roots of large oaks, huge planes, giant elms and assorted ash trees. As if it were not a path with almost every step inked in black on the chart of life.

Knut, aged seventeen months, happily tottering the same way with Mother, hardly ever skinning a knee. But at seventeen *years*, nerves like alternating current rushing from his toes to the roots of his hair; transmissions running wild into the air:

Mayday, Mayday.

Were the love gods on watch? Tuned to the frequency of the love light at the red end of the spectrum? Their mood softly inclined, favourably aspected, or colour-blind and tone deaf from the bone weariness of aeons of love and tenderness?

Might these gods be prepared to limit that ancient component of confusion to the minds and eyes of spies, gossips and inquisitors, leaving just enough over to confuse the young lady a little? Mildly, lovingly, gently. Withholding from her the understanding that the chills conveyed through the hand of her loved one were related to matters of his internal security. Were interdepartmental; wired by a remarkable short circuit to highly heated localised areas of excitement. Not that they were signalling anything dreadful, but rather they were due to Knut's inexperience in the more practical matters of love, to his lifelong and exhausting expectations, together with his adoration of this same young lady.

Nanette's hand was equatorial; a steam-heated hand; a woodfire stove. Unnerving. Exhilarating. Provoking wildly mixed metaphors and emotions like the gathering of a dazzling disarray of breathtaking blooms. Orchids. Violets. Peonies. Oldfashioned roses. A bunching of embarrassments bound with bold red ribbon.

Yet Nanette saw herself in almost every way as a well-puttogether young person; able to distinguish herself in class and look her peers in the eye. Physically, she was most satisfactorily assembled; less than stunning from only a couple of minor angles. Indeed, some of her more rewarding moments, aesthetically, were spent before the mirror when front door and back were latched and no one else was at home. And – allowing for the limits of her strength – well able to take care of herself as three young gentlemen, long on vanity but short on timing, might only on oath have admitted.

Hence, in the confusion and splendour of her bloom, in the company of her Knut, she was submissive in little ways on one day and haughty on another. Something to do with hormones. Or common sense. Or the influence of much loved grandmothers.

Hardly ever was she off the swings, all too often surprised not to have identified a moment of danger until it had passed. Intuition was telling her, just the same, that Knut might not have been as confident as he would have wished in view of his reputation that marched ahead of him like a Scots pipe band.

'Remember you're five feet one!' It was Nanette's mother who reminded her of it. 'A throwback, I fear, to our Cornishmen crawling through little tunnels in search of tin. Beside a boy built like a tank, you're a peashooter.'

'I'm a hundred and fifty-six centimetres tall!'

'A hundred and fifty-six centimetres small, my girl, and any day now, when you're looking some other way, the grown-up world may make the grab. Remember. You're warned.'

Nanette: hurrying beside her Knut; not at ease with her Knut; not accustomed to his mood; not liking it much; her thoughts and composure were breaking into fragments.

In lots of ways, Knut, you're my badge of pride. Everywhere we go I'm safe with you except when I'm alone with you. But that's all right. That's okay.

It's almost a year since you crossed the floor on your way to me.

I panicked. Knut Canute, straight from the fairytales, bowing to me, as if it were long ago and hundreds of years had vanished in a moment.

I was fifteen and over the moon and so frightened.

Tonight it's the same. But different. This dance of ours along streets where we grew up is coming too easy. Too simply. I'm troubled: I've never thought of being troubled in this way before and my parents will know if I let slip a single word out of place.

If they say to me, 'That boy's no good,' I'll never bear it. If they say, 'We've trusted you. We don't care about this year's fashion. You know the rules. We forbid you to leave the house in his company again.'

It's not like your house, my love. Mine is an old-fashioned family and there's no guarantee I'll dare to see it through. There's nothing in the stars I've agreed to. I said, 'We'll see. We'll see.'

If it's *no* that you hear from me, please, please, let it be. Don't shame me. Don't embarrass me.

The boys think every girl's got nothing else on her mind. Perhaps she hasn't. But it's not the same. Boys can be a problem, my love.

The gym mistress says, give them a knee. Don't mess around, she says. But don't blame them. They're programmed. They've been the same for thousands of years. That doesn't mean you have to entertain them if you're not in the mood.

I'd never give you the knee, my love. God knows what I'd do. As for Mum. She has this droll way of driving her point home. Not like *your* parents. They're too much for me. It's my Gran who does the trusting. And my Nan. But they get their points home, too. They tell me to be true to myself and to the one I love, but the truth can be known only to me.

I love you, my darling, I do. All my life I know I'll love you, but I'm different from others who've walked this way with you. Who probably loved you, too, but didn't have my Gran or my Nan.

Have you given thought to what it might be for someone whose defences are a peashooter? To the danger that lies between even the sweetest murmurs she hears? (My Gran). To know she can't expect to be in certain command? (My Nan). And it's Gran who says, 'The right one's out there. Searching. Just as you are. Don't be soured by talk of how hard they are or uncaring. You may pass him on the street. May not give a glance. May never see him again. Ever. Personal tragedies don't rate much higher with me. Think it through.'

Mum says, 'Follow your heart, but listen to me.'

Knut, who carries the wound if you walk away? The get-away is on your side. What hope have I against the strength and authority that sets you apart from everyone around?

My mum's not crash-hot on serious matters. Too fast with the ready word. I've heard her say that love isn't passion or lust: if it isn't trust it's a lemon.

GODS OF LOVE AND CONFUSION

Knut's thoughts about love and
his plan to spend the evening
with Nanette.

Are these gods Knut's demons? Or his fears, moods, imaginings?
They are his humanity.

Knut knew his princess Nanette came from the world where
mortals lived. Where people paid fares. Where one got born, got
on with it, then one day ran out of time.

Knut had a problem with mortality and another with immortality. Both scared him half to death.

In the real world life was practical. Was cash and carry. Was
made by the levelling of mountains, the elevating of plains and
the channelling of seas.

In the real world, one plus one made two. Two plus one made
awkward situations. Cats were fed at feeding time. Houses and
gardens were maintained or went back to the bush.

A proportion of the noble towers, the ziggurats, conceived in the
mind of Richard Canute – the great man, Knut's father – took
shape as he strode the length of Sebastian Street, down into the
gully and back to the top. There, narrowly and often, he

avoided death at various crossroads while his teenage slave Knut mowed lawns, weeded flower beds, serviced the hot tub and the fish pond and cleaned windows and roof gutters.

In the real world it cost to stand still, but cost more to go. It cost to have roof gutters, windows, fish ponds, hot tubs, flower beds and mown grass. Knut was not always convinced it was fair, yet he managed to make sure it cost his father plenty.

Citizens complained that every second breath cost more than they could afford. Thank God, they said, our bodies came free. Where, thought Knut, did they get that idea? Which was an advanced conclusion for a kid of seventeen. Advanced, ominous and prophetic.

From his private world it was necessary for Knut to descend an immense distance to Earth to deal with those of his peers who expected him to drink like a conger eel, sound off like a sewer, stagger when drunk like a stunned stoat, smell like a skunk, and present irrefutable evidence that he was the great lover with a waiting list.

It was to his darling Nanette that this heroic figure was driven to say, 'It's because I'm cold that I'm shivering. I'm sorry I'm shivering.'

He was *stricken* that he was shivering.

Well, winter was several weeks advanced. But it was not in any mood to deliver a bite, still gossiping (Mother might have said) with the last days of a loquacious autumn. Lovely word, *loquacious*, if only one knew what it meant.

In no way, on oath, would Knut have supported his assertion that he was cold, even if there were a few drops of rain. And Nanette glanced, with scarcely a question, towards the invisible Milky Way, for she was young enough and old enough to love gently and wildly and give her boy, now and then, a limited go, even if she couldn't believe half of what he had to say.

Hell, thought Knut, what's my *plan*?

Striving to recall its subtle details against his self-imposed rush along these tree-lined streets and fence-lined lanes, each tree and fence picket nudging its neighbour.

He should've written the plan in invisible ink on an invisible card and carried it next to the rib below which the signal fires burned. Should've committed it to memory and recited it in solitude. In the small, dark hours of each night he should have dreamt it. Impressing it. Imprinting it.

But of course he had. His dream was old hat. At six months or six years or sixteen: the dream of the beautiful maid.

The plan!

Knut foresaw a dim light, but not dull. Warm, as if from fire glow. Regretfully, fire glow was not on issue in his attic bedroom except in the event of calamity.

Thought Knut: who is it that strikes matches in our house to ignite his stinking cigar? But Father, we trust, is by now at the opera seeing *The Turn of the Screw*, grizzled head inclined towards Mother's right shoulder and Mother looking interesting in her Thai silk scarf, suitably worn like a gas mask. They were there to celebrate Conception Day, eighteen years gone.

Neither, thought Knut, shall there be in my attic room any visible point of light to draw the eye or the binoculars of any upper window, next door or over the crossroads. No light but the navigation light of the digital clock isolated in the magical, mystical glow on loan from that gorgeous red end of the spectrum, that glow of the night entering from city streets

11

through the slight parting of Knut's curtains already arranged, leaving no line open to any intruding eye, unless it be that of the owl. But, as widely known, the gentleman owl spies only upon other gentleman owls illicitly engaged.

The plan?

Knut's plan envisaged these several million collaborating points of light (originating close by or far distant) combining to create and sustain that most desirable red end of the spectrum. Blobs of light, beams of it, bands of it, escaping through windowpanes, coming around corners from candle-lit dining tables, torchlights, headlights, neons and fluorescents and incandescents and distant planets and moons and conveniently exploding stars without dependent planetary systems.

All combining, my darling Nanette, magically and mystically and discreetly for thee and me.

The lights of the unimaginable Universe marching in line abreast for this one sacred occasion, were committed to the creation of a soft awareness of each other for Knut and Nanette. A light for the sharing of sacred secrets; not for the display of mere commodities.

The plan?

Why was it so difficult to pursue a single thought in a direct line towards this numbing and stunning dreamland of a thousand and one nights? Year upon year, season upon season, moon upon moon, this luscious dreamland of love had gone on acquiring greater and greater refinement. Perhaps better expressed as development and intensification.

Well, there she was. The enchanting Nanette. Attached by the hand. Nailed by the paw. Grafted to the arm. The first female representative (unrelated by blood) to come out of the wide,

wide world in whom he'd felt able to lodge trust and longings and expectations.

Who would believe?

Did she?

The plan!

Why should the gods of the elements be so mean with air? What need had they of air? What could they do with it elsewhere? Where did it belong but here?

And what of downstairs at the corner of Sebastian and Johann Streets? What of the Canute residence there? Doors and windows, internal and external, sealed electronically to cover a mere half-million contingencies. Richard Canute's one-up security system. Knut would be well advised not to mislay his keys or confuse the codes. Flashing his free hand (on the brightly lit street) for the reassurance of the jingle in his pocket.

For these mercies, ten thousand times thank you!

Upstairs in wait, on call, the one visible source of light. The unblinking little red numerals. Alarm set? Check. To guard against any outflanking movement from the perilous force widely known as the deep sleep of the young and healthy. Against the possibility of this emergency, der clock is der guardian. Notably at 10.30 p.m. when it must sing like the devil.

Wake up, kids. Time to run.

The purr, the burrrrrr, the call at once to be stifled in the sacred almost-dark which will have shared all secrets, hopefully betraying none.

Knut's plan? To escape from the sacred chamber into the illuminated world hemming us about with souped-up eyes and ears in collusion with the last scene of *The Turn of the Screw*.

All evasive manoeuvres to be completed before the approach of the aged red Swedish tank under the command of Father, the celebrated Richard Canute, et cetera, et cetera, et cetera.

Now, thought Knut, am I able to say I've remembered my plan? What of aunts, cousins or survey takers ringing at the door? What of a mishap going up the stairs? Or coming down after?

What of routine misfortune? Nothing being more inventive or invasive than routine misfortune. What of accidents at the crossroads? What of kidney failure, toothache, power strikes, civil unrest, earthquake, flood, war? What if the hot water service blows up?

THE RIB BELOW
WHICH THE SIGNAL
FIRES BURN

*Knut and Nanette learn it is better
to hold hands and say nothing.*

Knut and Nanette were still on the streets, still getting there, still hastening short of the gallop, hands still clasped one to the other. Breathlessly, Knut said to Nanette: 'There's no need to run. It's under control. Everyone around here is a hundred years old. All you've got to do is *blend,* Mother says. That's your privacy around here, she says. Blend.'

Nanette: 'Am I running? Are you? The film we don't intend to see won't be out till 10.20 p.m. Then there's the alleged tram ride and the walk home. No one expects me to sprint. While you're moving, Mum says, everything's fine: 11.15 is an acceptable time. I don't plan to hurry now or then.'

Knut wasn't deliriously happy with the tone, the feel or the progression of events, but they were drawing closer by the stride to the side gate on Johann Street.

'It's all thought through,' he said. 'I've been checking as we've come. I've been planning it since I was twelve.'

Which wounded Nanette, as it always did. 'Really,' she said, 'I don't know why you stick to that line. Everyone's got faults.

15

You've got yours. A year ago you hadn't heard of me. Five years ago I was in fifth grade.'

'I say it over and over. You've been in my heart since I was twelve.'

'This line of yours wears me out. We both know how long we've known each other and it's not your heart that's on your mind.'

Beads of sweat, he could've sworn, were starting from his brow. Truly, truly he didn't expect perfection of his girl. He wished only for beauty. For innocence. For vivacity. For modesty. For joyfulness. For playfulness and a loving heart. Eagerness. Intelligence. Sensitivity. And an occasional, endearing streak of wildness.

It wasn't necessary for young ladies to be hewn out of granite. Young ladies, unlike young gentlemen, happened naturally, as all nice guys knew.

For Knut, an adequate supply of air was becoming more and more difficult to acquire.

He said, 'Look, no matter what, I've worked it through. It's covered.'

'The more you say the worse you make it!'

'Your part of the deal,' he said, very short on breath, 'is to look casual in public. No hesitation or anything. As if we're going to a church social. Nothing can go wrong if we keep calm. Why don't you trust me? Even if we fall asleep. Even if we get cornered, there's still a way out.'

'Out through the window? Across the roof? Down the drain pipe? Trailing our skirts and shirts behind us?'

'Nanette! You've heard the Volvo. Who hasn't? They'll circle the roundabout. They'll open the gate. Drive in. Close the gate.

Open the garage door while the engine put-puts and the fan belt squeaks. They switch off. Wait five seconds for the engine to stop. Search for programs, handbags, anniversary gifts and so on. Get out. Lock up. Defuse the alarm. Open the house door and stumble in. While *we* flash down the back stairs, out through the fernery and the side gate which'll be ready and waiting on the latch as it is now.'

Knut turned a private shade of grey. *I went out the front way! God, I'll bet you I've blown it. I'll bet you I've locked us out. We'll have to go round by the front to get into the house, in view of every spy in every upstairs window in the street.*

At which point Nanette presented the observation: 'Your regular get-away route, I suppose? Down the stairs? Out the side gate? And off lickety-split down the street?'

Knut needed a few paces for the point to hit the nerve. 'What's that supposed to mean?'

'What else? With the other girls.'

Knut beating at his right hip with his free hand, sweat starting from his armpits: 'I've told you there aren't any other girls.'

Hissing it. Because fences had ears, eyes and tongues. Fences knew who passed by, who paused, who dawdled, who ran. Fences reported upon everything.

Knut whispering: 'We're spoiling it.'

'*You're* spoiling it. You said they wouldn't be home till midnight. No way, you said. I remind you, Mr Canute, I've got grandmothers and they're a real big deal in the Baptists. I was doing fine till you started in on escape plans.'

If he'd swallowed a couple of teeth it might have been less serious.

...

The side gate; they were coming up under the yellow floodlights at the intersection of Sebastian and Johann; illuminating the miracle that Nanette and Knut were still side by side and hand to hand; that the gods of love and confusion had been relatively kind. So far.

Floodlights over the roundabout! They'd slipped Knut's mind. Their one remaining hope of invisibility; lightning and thunder striking everyone blind!

Knut was striding ahead, certain the gate would be locked, stepping across, whacking at the latch as he passed with a savagery of spirit and a heaviness of hand.

It opened.

Nanette darted through and he was after her.

They were there. Leaning against the inside with the world on the outside. And inside it was the night shade of garden trees, a hint of violets, and fences as dark as darkness might reasonably have been.

Her arms came slowly to his waist. She moved under his chin and quietly said, 'You know I'm your girl. How can you not know? But you gnaw at our nerves. It spoils our lovely time.'

He could've cried. 'But I *did* think it through. I've been working at it for so long. Always for you.'

'You shouldn't deny the others, Knut.'

'I do. I do.'

'I'm not jealous, my love. Girls talk.'

'There's nothing for them to talk about.'

'If you deny them, you'll deny me, too.'

Oh, God.

'I keep thinking, I hope my love's careful. Some of these

girls . . . They look like butter wouldn't melt . . . With me it's right. No tales told and none to tell . . . '

He said again: 'Knowing you or not knowing you, all my life, true to you. Except for one you can't count.'

'Cynthia? Your sister?'

'Come on, come on. You know Cynthia's never been born!'

'Knut, we're talking ourselves to death.'

LOVE CHILD

*Knut's birth, family, home,
special interests and his
remarkable door.*

Additional information relating to Knut Mannerheim Canute is here supplied:

His public image: from time to time he was addressed as Captain Canute. Occasionally as Master Canute.

'Good morning, Master Canute. How nice of you to call! How charming.'

'Good morning, Aunt Sophie. Good morning, Aunt Ingrid. Isn't this just the perfect day?'

'Always is, Knut dear, when you come by.'

'Always is, Aunt Ingrid, when you open the door side by side. How do you know I'm on the way?'

'How do you know that muffins are just out of the oven? And morning coffee's on the brew? How do you know and how do we? What's the nature of the mystery?'

'My life,' said Knut to all the world, 'is one long perfect day.'

The same young man might be addressed by less mature female persons as Mister Canute. These several young ladies (some known, others unidentified) sharing the illusion that by uttering his name in his presence with intensity, but silently, a

bewitchment in Arthurian style might embrace the leading play-
ers, rendering all guiltless and conveying them to the blissful
realm of dreams fulfilled.

'Good morning, Mister Canute,' significantly more than one
young lady had been known to say.

'Hello, there. Hello, you. I don't think we've met. Well, it
doesn't matter. We've met now.'

Fantasy followed the steps of Mister Canute. Opportunities
for improper behaviour besieged him, but were wasted upon
him, one must suppose.

In the first instance, Knut was a love child. This was received as
an appalling item of intelligence by family connections those
several years ago.

'I'm shocked beyond belief!' Great Aunt Sophie said, seven
months before the birth of the brat. 'There's nothing further I
can say. The concept is inconceivable.'

'Most shocking,' agreed Great Aunt Ingrid, wistfully, 'but not
inconceivable, Sophie dear. That's not the word, I fear.'

It's been said that wistfulness is the nature of Ingrid. Her bus
disappears around the corner as she approaches, or arrives as
she walks for the next stop. Her size at the sales? Trade regula-
tions must somehow exclude it.

Knut Canute. Unnamed at that point, but all too soon the all
too visible outcome of Ms Madeleine Mannerheim's remarkable
indiscretion in her thirty-sixth year:

Our Ms Mannerheim sat on the wall,
Our Ms Mannerheim had a great fall,

All the king's horses and all the king's men
Said half your luck, mate;
What's the magic formula?

This was the year marked by the lady's early resignation from Wittenburg College due to ill health, a technicality in lieu of what others might have called an obvious diagnosis.

'At her age,' Great Aunt Sophie said, 'a blue stocking like her? Her sainted mother would've dropped dead.'

'Her sainted mother *did* drop dead, Sophie dear. Trying to climb the Matterhorn. As I'm sure you recall.'

'I have no difficulty with recall, Ingrid. Or with the irony of bracketing her mother with the saints. Now, this daughter, this supposed language teacher of young gentlemen, appointed upon *our* recommendation, this plain Jane . . . '

'That's not necessary, Sophie dear. Madeleine is most competent. As widely acknowledged. And of pleasing countenance.'

'This plain Jane . . . Aged thirty-five . . . In *our* Lutheran College, Ingrid! Upheld by our intellectual input, material endowments and worldly wisdom. Now I hear she's written a book. About what may be an imprudent question. Did I not say that gallivanting in the snow shall always be much too much in the Swiss tradition? About which everyone in the family knows.

'Fifteen young gentlemen, Year Twelve, in Madeleine's care. Dear, dear. Left to their own devices, one must suppose. To mimic the example of their chaperone. There lies a page, Ingrid, unwise to turn. An instructional weekend in the mountains would never have been approved by *our* sub-committee. What manner of instruction, pray?'

'It was very cold, Sophie dear.'

'*What* was?'

'The night upon which she wrote the book.'

'Am I the universal fount, Ingrid? Am I to see into the echoing chambers of your mind?'

'He might well have assisted her.'

'He assisted her beyond a doubt!'

'The two beside the midnight fire in the alpine lodge. Snowflakes pattering against the windowpane ...'

'Snowflakes, sister, do not patter.'

'Perhaps he went forth into the blizzard of snow, torrential rain and continuing pattering hail, to chop the wood to keep the flames dancing until dawn, inspiring and sustaining her muse. The spirit of the family. The spirit of our creativity. If she writes a book, it's partly ours.'

'You need to keep the hole in your head covered, sister, or someone will fall in it! No one writes a book overnight.'

'Mr Wallace, Sophie, did so with his crime stories on several occasions as is well known in literary circles.'

'Mr Wallace was a common little man who frequented race-tracks and owed money all over the place and had little to do with literary circles and nothing to do with any branch of our family. We exorcised the Wallace connection years ago.'

Knut Canute. Birth achieved.

Page 1 of the *Evening News*.

LOVE CHILD.

Arresting photograph 125 mm deep by four columns wide trimmed to three columns by 90 mm for later editions. Knut clasped in the bared arms of shell-shocked mother; mother clasped in the arms of father as if all had just come in from a hard-fought match on a hard-surfaced court on a hot afternoon to deal with this extraordinary occurrence:

Hail to the first-born of April Fool's Day.

Baby Canute.

To controversial lovers Madeleine Mannerheim and the famous Richard. Pictured in St George's at eleven minutes past twelve this morning.

Whereupon Aunt Sophie delivered judgement:

'Ingrid, I say, especially, do not condemn our girl. God forbid we should sink in the mud of conformity. The world we knew isn't the world we have. Join the century, dear. Here we have the classic love child. First male among the Mannerheims in forty years. The stuff that pretenders to the throne were made of. Ingrid, that father of his! That man. That gorgeous man. Pray our boy grows to fill his shadow.'

Knut filled it.

In due course, KMC (Knut Mannerheim Canute) acquired regional note in his own right as the wild-haired kid at the corner of Sebastian and Johann Streets.

'My hair,' he said at 'Show and Tell' in Year Four, 'is virtually uncontrollable. In Mother's opinion it's to be preferred to an uncontrollable temper. Not exactly red. Father describes it as neither carrot nor claret. More in the nature of chestnuts, he says, among the coals of an autumn evening.'

Only child as well.

'My parents,' Knut explained in Year Five in 'My Family and I', 'feared they'd not strike gold twice. A sadness for me. Or I'd have had my Cynthia, my beautiful sister at my side. But I can only dream of my Cynthia and me, for she has never been born.

I do wonder if she's out there somewhere, in some other family, called Mary Murphy or Connie Constantine?'

This kid, this Knut, for whatever reason, thus became the sole issue of the resident lovers in the fey-looking house at the southeast corner of the crossing of Sebastian and Johann streets.

It was a well-known house, dating from 1865, that could be passed at high speed in four directions by the more immortal drivers of probationary licence age. Leaving in their wake an alarming blast, quantities of irritated senior citizens and occasional wrecks of avoidance wrapped about the fire hydrant adjacent to the Canute front gate.

'Our fire hydrant,' the famous Richard said, 'is part of the national estate. Cast iron. Of enormous weight. And noble age, as of this date. I shall be very bloody cross if it suffers metal fatigue in the course of these assaults. God save the yahoo who remains in reach of me on the day I find it in a fractured heap.'

Richard, red-hot poker in thickly gloved hand, burnt his statement in brief into a hardwood plank secured by round-headed bolts to the front fence.

This was the period when tow truck operators left visiting cards in letterboxes within impact range of the corner. *Do give us a call. We'll see you right if we get here first.*

'Not,' Richard said, 'if I see you first.'

The roundabout, dating from more recent times, introduced new intensity to a combat already refined. And the advanced black locust tree, planted in a spasm of optimism by the local authority at the centre of the roundabout, protected by a grid of used railway sleepers and several tonnes of recycled bluestone blocks, did in fact attain a kind of bent maturity.

At intervals, attired in his studious attitude, young Canute sat in his attic bedroom window, legs crossed, regulation clipboard in lap, crunching on those blatantly yellow cheese things (stomach like a stainless steel expansion tank), counting road vehicles as they negotiated the hub of the intersecting streets.

Over several years Knut witnessed five robust collisions and struck an average of one vehicle passing through every six point eight seconds, without notified loss of life, based on samples taken at random between 7.20 a.m. and 6.30 p.m. Monday to Friday, excluding public holidays and semester breaks.

'Impossible,' Father said.

'Utterly, utterly out of the question,' Father said, 'though I do not dispute the contributing lunacy of your contemporaries who remind me so strongly of *Homo erectus*. Your study, child, is unscientific. Our district is famous, nay, *notorious* for outergalactic peace and quiet, which hangs so heavily that even I submitted to the blessed oblivion of residential status. For confirmation, refer to your mother who remembers all things except the time of day and the recipe for boiled eggs. As is common knowledge, everyone hereabouts, excluding us, is unborn or partly dead of natural causes.'

Knut, in response, presented his detailed report.

'Sir. With respect and with your permission. Dedicated to you with filial affection. I present my first serious study based on four hundred and seventy-three collective samples taken at random over sixty-one consecutive calendar months, excluding Januaries.'

'Why no Januaries?'

'Everyone on holidays, sir.'

'Continue.'

'Of the ninety-eight thousand three hundred and fourteen

vehicles observed, pushbikes, child-sized tricycles and perambulators excluded, percentages are as follows: private cars – forty-eight point two per cent. Station wagons – eleven point six per cent. Four plus fours with bull-bars – fourteen point one per cent. XK 120s, MGs, Morgans, Austin-Healeys – point zero zero zero of one per cent. Ambulances – two per cent. Hearses – two per cent. Fire brigades – zero per cent. Police cars – zero per cent. Search and Rescue . . . '

'Silence,' said Father.

'I haven't finished, sir.'

'To the contrary!'

'I haven't reported the substance, sir, of several severe collisions observed. Illuminating.'

'Do I wish to be illuminated?'

'Notably, the impact of Mr Aberdeen Angus in his Suzuki Hatch with the fully laden garbage truck.'

'Mr Aberdeen *what*?'

'Angus, sir. The spilled garbage was cleared by six men in two hours, eleven minutes. A bore, sir. Really, sir. Ruined my Tuesday.'

'Why were you not at school?'

'Appendix, sir.'

'Why were you not in hospital?'

'No bed, sir?'

'My son waiting on a bed?'

'I survived, sir. You were in Singapore. Shall I proceed with my account of the truck?'

'What truck?'

'The garbage truck, sir. Righted by a mobile crane and towed away. Mr Aberdeen Angus drove home.'

'In a two per cent hearse?'

'No, sir. In the aforesaid Suzuki Hatch.'

'Fiddlesticks. Further, your totals don't add up.'

'The requirements of science have been met, sir, as I will prove.'

'Silence,' said Father, 'is golden. Science of your kind is another matter. Go walk the gorilla.'

'We haven't got a gorilla.'

'Go find one. It'll take but a moment. Try old buggerlugs next door.'

'After six years of applied labour, sir, a longed-for objective, the presentation of my study to you . . . Are you declining my dedication? Are you telling me to go to Hell?'

'Did I say that?'

'Not in as many words, sir.'

'Did I say it in any number of words?'

'If one must split hairs; no, sir.'

'Then why bloody ask?'

'Because, for the moment, I bear a wound, sir.'

It appeared to be the moment in which Knut found himself crushed to the great man's chest.

A local identity showing around friends from abroad had been overheard: 'That's the Canute house. His and hers. Take a look at it if you can bear it. A man of his achievement living in a house like that? What one does for passion.'

But there was nothing strange or censurable about Knut's agreeing to live there, taking into account a reasonable level of implied parental pressure and plain commonsense. A roof that wouldn't dare leak habitually. Helpful, when obvious drip points were close to one's scalp. Useful reference library addressed to varied subjects, but in no way the customary clutch of family volumes with supplements and yearbooks. Around six thousand units at the last count. Even a hot tub, lovely smell of cedar, scene of numerous summer imaginings after dark from age twelve onwards, even if unavailable in winter.

'Do you think I'm bloody made of money? Of course I'm not starting up the tub to humour a precocious child. Go fill the hand basin from the hot tap and stick your head in it.'

Interesting table, evening by evening. Virtually free of charge, apart from the periodic sprint to the corner shop for critical ingredients on closing time. This was noted more keenly by Knut, with the awakening of enthusiasms, after he turned thirteen.

A cuisine, especially Szechwan, but Thai, French, Italian and Vietnamese. Notably when Father was at home. Generous on garlic. Heavy on chilli. Hardly ever British, except for roast beef with a sublime Yorkshire pudding.

Marginal tolerance of teenage fads, fashions and furies. Excluding mutilation at the hairdressers.

Knut had an attic room with a magnificently conceived sound-proofed door, signed, bottom left corner, KMC. A big deal. Ceiling on the low side; a little hot in summer, but nothing that selective nudity didn't make endurable.

What more might one reasonably expect of parents born at such distantly early dates?

'Father. A question. Your age?'

'You know my age. I've been telling you for years.'

'It always stays the same.'

'If you take a child bride, so will yours.'

'Mother was thirty-five!'

'Agreed. What's the argument?'

On the authority of *Who's Who*, this man, at the latest reckoning, would need to be seventy-two. One might as well have been sired by Chaplin.

Whereas Mother remained scrumptiously notorious. Notably at school, where they said, 'They reckon your mother's the teacher who got expelled for immoral behaviour.'

'Do they reckon that?' said Knut.

'Do you deny it?'

'Why would I do that?'

'Is it true you're the result of the immoral behaviour!'

'If I'm not, I'll be very disappointed.'

CHAPTER
FIVE

SPIRITS IN TRANSIT

Matters relating to Knut's
accomplishments and the
emergence of a serious
problem.

Some have said that the house at the corner of Sebastian and Johann Streets where Knut once lived has become a bloody-minded house, unwilling to settle for less than its lost golden age.

Coming first, after the Canutes had gone, was the large gentleman with the bow tie, the white carnation and the gas-fired barbecues for business associates, politicians, foreign delegations and ladies of strong nerve. The house was constantly misbehaving: alarm system inviting police invasions, sewers disgorging into bathrooms, violets and helleborus along the side fence to Johann wilting in the vapours of barbecues, whereas Knut's long feet and runaway mower had stimulated growth.

Problems of another kind came with someone's elderly widowed mother and her supporting Cavalier King Charles spaniels. Around a dozen bedding down to each main room; four to the broom cupboard. Even the kookaburras moved out of the garden. Eventually, the widowed lady moved out also, assisted by the elbow of a compassionate local authority. 'Two dogs, madam. That's the law.' And restful nights for her had been rare; walls still bearing the shadows of pictures not there; and not for sensitive old bones was that odd attic room from which a door had been removed at the top of the stairs.

Her successor stayed but five months, whilst driving his Merc from fun parlour to massage parlour picking up his hard-earned loot. Perhaps his choice of house had been influenced by the new wife who believed she'd married a restaurateur. His departure immediately followed hers.

Epochs come, it is said. And go. Which, for reasons not fully understood, may continue to be the way for the house wherein Knut took his first steps, sang his first simple songs about twinkling stars and contrary Marys and swore his first fierce ringing oaths.

'Oh, blast. Oh, blither. Oh, bother. Oh, *Mother*!'

This was the house from which Knut was conducted by the celebrated Madeleine, his mother, on foot or by ageing Swedish station wagon, to kindergarten in the morning shadow of the Mediterranean-styled church down the road; then to the local primary school a few steps further in the opposite direction, and, subsequently (even by Father), to that excellent secondary college for young gentlemen those several kilometres closer to town.

'No,' said the headmaster when he first met Knut (though out of Knut's hearing), 'impossible, madam, as you must know. Take him elsewhere, please. There are many good schools. The landscape barely supports their weight.'

'Your splendid school, Headmaster, is his father's choice. Nothing but Wittenburg College will do. Would you refuse the only son of Canute because he happens to be my son also? Described by his primary school principal as outstanding on the playing field and creative in class. Are you to turn him away? Are you to live with your regrets? Have you considered your explanations to the media?'

'You wouldn't threaten me, madam!'

'News is news, headmaster. Our household attracts its purveyors. Confidently, Richard and I are inviting you to participate in the making of a leader who may contribute to the sum of human achievement.'

This house, too, was the crucible wherein Knut conceived his interesting traffic survey, achieved a notable number of almost wholesome imaginings – and stumbled in after dark through the side gate on that deliciously terrifying occasion in the company of his sweet Nanette, part French, part Irish, part Cornish, but almost wholly antipodean.

Yes. When Mother and Father on their annual festive outing were attending *The Turn of the Screw* at such enormous expense there was no likelihood of their return before eleven and an acceptable chance they'd not be in before one, two or three in the morning of July 4.

And tragically for them, they were not.

By whatever name, the young Canute earns his place as almost everyone's down-the-middle-of-the-track good guy. Born with brain and charm. With significant muscle, agility, accuracy and speed; a serious performer with the foil. An odd mix of talents that included the gift of the gab and in moments of need a momentous shortage of luck that gladdened the hearts of his enemies. Suggesting he might be destined to become a victim and that the intersection of Sebastian and Johann might not always be the pleasant scene that it appeared to be while he was there.

In the end, it was as if he, like Cynthia, had never been born. As if his parents, who cherished him, had not met long ago in the snow and celebrated for the eighteenth time on the curious night of *The Turn of the Screw*.

And, from time to time, the unknown or occasionally glimpsed young ladies who had adored him, sobbed into their pillows with variations on the theme: 'Woe to them, Knut, if they've harmed you. Woe, whoever they are, whatever they be.' And what greater woe may befall the human head than the invocation of the wounded maid?

Great Aunt Sophie said, 'Our darling boy. What have they done with him? Who, who would do such a wicked thing to such a beautiful boy? To snatch him away. To leave not a clue and not a word.'

Great Aunt Ingrid said, 'He was the child of love. One of God's own? Where were his guardians and his angels?'

At a later time by several weeks, Ingrid said, 'Sophie . . . That night Knut went with me to the Anglers' Hall. You recall? Two years or so ago. And we missed the last train home.'

'Yes. Yes?'

'I had not responded to a general notice of the lecture. Nothing like that. My invitation came over the signature of Phillip Hann.'

'The archaeologist?'

'Yes, Sophie.'

'To *you*? In person?'

'Yes, my dear. I fear so. Making mention of Richard's

ziggurats and his hope that Richard's son, Knut, would accompany me. The honour of it, Sophie. Such a man writing to me. The letter addressed personally from England.'

'You haven't mentioned this before, Ingrid. Not a breath of it. Why, indeed *how* would Hann have known of you, or of your connection with Richard?'

'It didn't occur to me at the time, Sophie.'

'But why keep it from me at all? How irregular of you. I understood Knut went with you for company. Because of the distance. Because it was night.'

'I told Knut the same. It wasn't an untruth. And I hoped it would make for a lovely surprise. Which it did, believe me. There was no audience but us.'

'Ingrid. You dismay me. More and more you dismay me. This could be important. This could be critical. For pity's sake! Why haven't you told me before?'

'It was Knut's night. And mine. A wonderful, wonderful night that we kept to share. But now ... But now ... '

'In the light of events, you mean?'

'No, Sophie. More.'

'What *more*, Ingrid?'

'Now I learn that Hann died in Haifa during the Gulf War. Months *before* the lecture in the Anglers' Hall. So who was it that we saw? Everything about him rang true. He was the image of the man I'd seen on film so many times before.'

'Ingrid. Oh, Ingrid dear. What has happened here? Ingrid, Ingrid, Hann must be the missing link. The reason for it all. What else, that Hann has been impersonated very cleverly indeed? Who was it that you saw? We must go immediately. Now. There are persons who must be told.'

MORE ABOUT THE PERFECT DAYS

Concerning, mainly, the celebrated Madeleine.

Historically, marginally, more about the house with the green shingles, the gables, the ornate ridges, the mossy slates, the lead-lighted windowpanes with tulips and wrought-iron lace. The house with the black London taxi cab in the side garden to Johann Street.

'A bloody Austin,' Father said. 'How come Jaguar didn't build a couple?'

In the good old days the cab was occasionally observed with Knut at the wheel. National Champion, Intermediate Foil, driving a cab on blocks? Indeed. From time to time he encouraged non-paying passengers to join him, the noted Madeleine among them; known locally among the less religious as the Dam of Knut. To be observed, with a rose-coloured clipboard in hand, writing her next book about murders of passion in Mayfair or another immortal item for small children concerning the infamous doings of the absolutely terrible, absolutely frightful, absolutely infamous Cootamundra Wattle Gnomes, inspired, no doubt, by the Scandinavian trolls.

She was a lady born to be English, it has been said, though of

36

solid Nordic descent and sentenced in childhood by the eccentricity of restless parents to the realities of the Congo and the Sahara, to islands of the south seas and to the rigours of British outer-colonial experience. Having grown up in a boarding school in a distant southern city called Melbourne. A sadness confirmed by the prolonged absences of parents only occasionally seen in the company of each other.

Kids who went for Knut called him King. 'Hey, King. What's your mum's next book? Is it sexy?'

'Why ask me?'

'You've got your finger on it, haven't you? All you've got to do is flip the page.'

'I'd suggest you ask her yourself. Just make sure you're running past real fast when you put the question. Beautiful women have got terrible tempers. And you know what the gnomes are like! Take your eyes off 'em and they take your head off.'

Well, almost everyone knew the gnomes in Madeleine's books had the most numerous collection of heads in fairyland. Largely of prime ministers, police sergeants, prima donnas, school principals and parents of children in boarding schools. Strong-minded people, these gnomes.

Kids who didn't go for Knut called him the bastard.

Which Knut shrugged off, but he felt a wound within. He would not have minded if they had said it with affection.

IMAGES IN THE
MIRROR

A sad story of Nanette De L'isle.

Knut's perfect days: what manner of person in his small corner escaped the news they had come to a close? A very small corner it would need to be.

Perhaps the hermit in the cave, if caves and hermits were in vogue that year?

Or the girl in the mirror?

Or the boy on the river bank strumming the bruised guitar, dreaming of the girl in the mirror?

Even the scholar of predetermined mind, papering the walls of his ivory tower with consternations?

Few others, it appears.

Truth may not be readily accessible to humans, to participants, eyewitnesses, judges and juries. Truth may resemble the vanishing image in the mirror. When the subject steps aside, when the light goes out, the image has gone. To where? Nor may one be sure that the Everlasting Eye at the Centre of All enjoys an unobstructed view of the subject either. And what is one to say of the belly belches of information, the newspaper headlines, upon which opinions are formed, judgements arrived at, reputations made or dismembered, and scriptures written to endure for thousands of years?

Truth, relative to Knut Canute, is a matter of which more, shortly, shall be recorded. Nothing suspected shall not be aired. Nothing felt will be ignored. Nothing known shall be left unsaid, for the nature of this document is its awareness of the issue as a whole. As facts or issues have become apparent, they have been recorded in the order of their discovery or understanding. Hence, from time to time, full understanding (like all revelation) comes along behind; is seen from a distance; or suddenly dawns. Upon these fundamental truths, this document stands or falls.

In the meantime, through the medium of newspaper headlines current at that time, let us confront all that the world at large was ever to know about the fate of Knut Mannerheim Canute. For the moment, we shall be no better informed than they.

NIGHT SMASH: YOUTH MISSING
CANUTE SON: FOUL PLAY?
CANUTE BED: FORENSIC TESTS
KNUT'S BED: UNEASY LAY THE HEAD
CANUTE CASE DISTURBS POLICE
KNUT SEEN DRUNK: WITNESS
CANUTE: POLICE VISIT SCHOOLS
KNUT: GREAT LOVER, STUDENTS SAY
KNUT A DROP-OUT: POLICE THEORY
KNUT: GAY, SAY GIRLS
RICHARD CANUTE DOES HIS BLOCK
ALLEGATION: KNUT PUSHED DRUGS
CANUTE FAMILY AND INTERPOL

CANUTE AUNTS ASSAULT POLICE
CANUTE AUNTS REFUSE BAIL
RICHARD CANUTE IN CUSTODY
QUEEN MADELEINE RULES IN COURT
POLICE APOLOGY TO CANUTE FAMILY
TIME, TIDE AND KNUT CANUTE

What of Nanette De L'isle?

The first evening, after the uproar began, Tuesday, July 4, her mother said: 'We have a problem, darling, that you need to think about. I can see that you have heard that Knut Canute has a problem, too.'

On the second evening, her mother said, 'This lad. This Knut Canute. He'll turn up, of course, I hope, for everyone's sake. But what have you to tell me in the meantime? Where does my Nanette fit?'

On the third day: 'I trust we're not heading for the third degree, my sweet, but I can't protect you if I don't know the truth. I'll make no judgements, I promise you. The film you went to see. You'd seen it already. Were you at the cinema? Or were you not?'

On the fourth day, she said, 'His parents called. His father is a difficult man. They were followed and were not pleased about it. Neither was I. I told them Knut brought you back at the arranged hour and treated us both with striking courtesy. I said the claim that he was drunk was absurd. I have been obliged, even commanded, to give this information to the police.'

On the sixth day, she said, 'You love this poor boy, don't you?'

On the seventh: 'Was he your first love, darling? Your special love? Your one and only. Believe me, as unlikely as it seems, love will come again.'

But it did not.

On the eighth day she said: 'I can't shield you from the media, but you must not allow them to destroy him for you. For them, all too often, it's only the story that counts.'

On the twenty-second day: 'He was a good lad. By so many excesses and absurdities the media has declared it for us. Which makes it very sad. I'm reminded, repeatedly, of great mysteries I've encountered in my ordered reading. Day by day, my brave girl, I pray he may come back, but I live in fear. We face it as a family. We will not allow it to wreck your life.'

It changed her life. Radically. At twenty-six years of age she was ordained.

As for her Knut, he never left her heart. She remained a virgin.

As for Knut himself, she was his great, great loneliness. Even when he was unable to understand anything else, he lived with the loneliness.

OTHER SIDES OF
THE BRAIN

*Knut is awakened from a deep
sleep. Or possibly not.*

Knut was seventeen by three months and a few days when a sound like thunder on a beach broke through the edges of his sleep. Sound effects or sounds of life, human and non-human, stuffed level upon level into the bottom of the brain. The brain protested: 'Bloody Hell to this.'

Knut giving attention to the problem. 'I'm dreaming. I should be purring like a kitten. All this racket is a parental plot to drag me back from the marvels observed at the rosy red end of the spectrum.'

Knut tried sliding back into the depths, reaching for his adorable maid. His darling girl. *Why* was she not there? What calamity had befallen the spectrum?

Knut's recollection: Life, according to Father, being long and Earth being large, the wise young person always leaves open a few options at all times and refrains from undisciplined vigour in dreams and fantasies, thus not arousing the hostility of the more narrow-minded gods, those of the pharisaic element of all religions and all heresies.

These gods, Father said. These gods. These aspects of one's humanity.

The maids of Earth, Father also said, though being without number, were never to be confused with statistics like motor cars at the intersection of Sebastian and Johann. Don't bog down in these bloody boring statistics, Father said. Maids were not meant for the mathematical side of the brain. Consider, Father said, my age as it's rumoured to be. I, wise, even when clasped to the bosom of my baby-feeding bottle, have had an eternity to become a sage.

This maid, this Nanette, this dream of mine, dreamt Knut, commands especial status among the greater works of art. Much to be preferred to the perplexing visions of the masters.

This maid. This dream who declares she is mine. Female and feline. Her cunning. Mockery. And wiles. Her tragedy. Her tenderness. Her bewildering laughter. Her possibilities equalled only by her shyness. Her shyness equalled at heart only by mine.

Knut, desperately, was holding to the dream.

'You're wonderful,' someone said, one or the other, or both.

'I love you, I love you.'

'Not one little bit more than I've loved you from the beginning of time.'

Thousands of volts were illuminating the attic room, emanating from human extremities, supplementing the gorgeous, rosy red end of the spectrum.

'My sweetheart.'

'My adored one.'

'How beautiful you are.'

'How precious. So precious. I could eat you.'

'Please. Please do.'

'Where did you come from? What did the Great God make you from?'

'Puppy dog tails and sour cream.'

'Oh fiddle-de-dee.'

'Out of Mum and Dad, I suppose. Darling Knut, out of what did He make you?'

'Search me and see. It all comes free. This week's special.'

A long pause.

Tears and a shaking as of nerves, his and hers.

She said: 'A voice says no.'

He said: 'Don't believe it. It's subversive. It's fallacious. You're allowed.'

She said: 'It's too soon.'

He said: 'It's a year.'

She said: 'It's ten months.'

He said: 'It's been for ever.'

She said: 'The voice inside says it's too soon.'

He said: 'My darling; my darling. Bloody Hell. We're living now. Now, now. Who knows what tomorrow may bring?'

How could these two female persons, Madeleine and Nanette, each so difficult and so different, so overwhelm the days and nights of one young man?

At the break of each working day, the elder of the two sat sagging against a door frame, in tune with the limp cornflakes, the burnt toast and the 'boiled' egg. A solid egg because she'd forgotten to take it off or liquid because she'd forgotten to ignite the gas.

Father protesting: 'Damn it, Madeleine. Egg nog again. One

44

of these mornings you'll blow us up. Start the day with a cold shower or at least stand clear until we've mounted our steeds and ridden off.'

'All right for you, Father. I can't ride off if Mother stays in bed.'

'You can walk.'

'Six kilometres!'

'Your great grandmother, Catherine Canute, walked two-and-a-half miles to school across worked-out goldfields and home again every day for the eight years then considered necessary to educate the young female.'

'How far, Father, did you walk to school?'

'That's irrelevant.'

At 7.40 a.m. Mother was not to be found at a level of consciousness that created the culinary experiences of an evening. Or of crushing responses, either.

Knut found himself to be darting in and out and around the edges of wakefulness at an hour entirely foreign to him.

I keep telling myself, he said, that sirens don't happen at the corner of Sebastian and Johann. How could war have been declared? War against whom? Mars? Outer Galactica? Troops heading for the front taking the wrong turning. Why?

We don't have wars down here even between the angels and the archangels. We love each other. We settle it man to man and woman to woman with boots and bricks and broom handles and bicycle chains.

So we have well-greased wheelchairs of a Sunday morning propelled by the aged and infirm and quiet consultations at street corners about whether the devil-may-care vicar will go for hymn 312 or 415 or a top-up of Tia Maria.

Knut went on clinging to the phantom image of his enchanting Nanette, gorgeous beyond belief in the extraordinarily intimate rosy red end of the spectrum; grinding his teeth and ordering his eyes to open in the supposed direction of the clock acquired at Christmas in the year he turned ten!

'Please, Mummay, may I have a digital clock for Christmas Day?'

'Have one now. There's one in the shed.'

'That won't do, Mummay.'

'For heaven's sake why not, honey-bunny?'

'It won't go.'

'Does it need to go? What's time to you?'

'Time's life, Mummay. I need to know I'm alive.'

'You have a watch. It'll give you the second, the minute, the hour, the day, the month and the north pole. Why don't you wind it up and observe the wondrous events that then occur?'

'I swapped my watch for the sundial. You said it'd be a good swap if Barry's dad didn't turn up with a pickaxe. But I can't trust it at night. When I shine my torch on it, it keeps changing its mind.'

'You're not awake at night.'

'Akela tells me there'll come a dark time when I will be and, like a good Wolf Cub, I must be prepared.'

'Is it any wonder,' Mother said, 'we didn't have a Cynthia?'

1.17 on the face of the little digital clock. Red and fuzzy. As if curious fogs had gathered in his head. As if he were not really there, but undoubtedly was. As if in limbo, but still hanging around. Whilst out there were raised voices, clatter, wailing, swearing, and the impact as if of torrential rain against his windowpane.

A raucous female person was shrieking, 'It's the ****** fire brigade, chum. Strike me ****** dead, we called for the ****** police. You heard me, chum!'

Knut was wincing and thinking: she must be one of those Billingsgate persons, those fishwife persons of whom parents speak. Where's my clipboard? I must make a note of these items while they're fresh in the mind; before I forget.

Where, by the way, is Billingsgate? And where's the gazetteer? Mother, you've pinched my clipboard again and stolen the gazetteer which I must in future remember to keep under the pillow. You never know when the need is about to arise. Maybe I should do away with the pillow and replace it with dictionary, street directory, compendium of quotations, thesaurus, atlas, gazetteer *and* encyclopaedia, all in soft-bound editions.

Fire brigade?

Is it reasonable to suppose we've cracked our zero per cent at last after all these years of amassing statistics? But in the middle of a rainstorm? Or a hailstorm? Or a meteoric shower?

Let's trust we're not ourselves at the centre of this curious event. If so, apart from me, what do I save first? Grandmother's portrait, Grandfather's diary, or my statistical survey of the crossroads, complete but for this present mishap?

You down there, sweetheart; you, with the voice like the back end of an orbital sander and vocabulary to match. You've no chance of securing the participation of the boys in blue. No cop has passed this way except when lost, or by chance, out of uniform, off duty, in his girlfriend's Capri, on his way to the local Oriental for a stir-fried fix, since I turned six. And I'm the one who'd know.

And what ambulance would come before ten in the morning,

even to revive the dead? Everyone round here dies of old age, at leisure. They never know they're dead and occasionally have been seen to rise again and wander off into the never-never land singing nursery rhymes and national anthems and that sort of thing.

Nor does this sweet voice I hear have anything to do with Mother returning at the end of a long night out. Mother never profanes and never filthies. Mother never calls anyone *chum*. Father, she calls dear heart. Me, she calls honey-bunny. Occasionally Knut. As for the rest of the humans, *dahling*. Particularly those that she and the human race would prefer to see dead.

'Mother! What's happening in the street?'

No answer from Mother, despite the magnitude of the bellow.

'Father! You must have an opinion.'

Father had opinions on everything. But none on this.

Which, thought Knut, indicates that the persons addressed are not yet home from *The Turn of the Screw*.

A curious choice for a night of celebration. Is it an opera, a wood-working class, or rude? Leaving the innocent boy unattended and defenceless. Exposed to the perils of a sinful night.

I really must not get out of bed. I could be morally at risk.

Whereas, did I not convey, I regret to say, my sweet Nanette, intact by her own certification, to her own front door at 11.15, bowing respectfully to the maternal figure?

'Thank you, ma'am. I appreciate enormously the company of your enchanting daughter. I hope you may permit me the pleasure again.'

Nanette's mother was massaging her stretched throat.

'Enchanting? Nanette, incline your head. More to the left, darling. Say something, Nanette. Can you think of anything enchanting? And may you, dear Bill, have the pleasure again? Strike while the iron's hot. Make the appointment while you stand in good stead.'

Bill?

Knut shook Nanette by the hand.

'Goodnight, dear Nanette. I hope you enjoyed the film.'

Who's this bloody Bill?

All this came directly upon our supposed attendance at a new-wave Russian film much admired by us for purely aesthetic reasons. Notably, the male and female leads in their more electrified moments. How these Russians have come on in recent years.

I recall my initial appreciation of the female protagonist as whispered into Nanette's edible left ear. 'She's lush.' But that was not last evening. No. I fear not so.

'He's a god,' I heard back from her, in my edible right ear. But that was not heard this last evening either. No jolly fear. None but a full month ago, and, enchanting Nanette, it remains a film we must see again in the absence of fire, riot and Bill.

What might my elderly parents be up to?

Supper at Susannah's indeed! Grossly improper behaviour. Notably from Father, whose antiquity is confirmed by the date of construction and his signature as architect on the so-called ziggurat in the middle of town. And who, long since, should have developed a proper disdain of mere physical pleasures and a greater sense of responsibility towards his only officially registered offspring, which, as far as I know, I am.

...

Father's ziggurat. Neo-Babel, to say the least of it. Several score storeys of exotic building materials, stacked up, level upon level, and crowned by a massive block of lapis lazuli to which lightning felt a striking attachment. To wit, the photographs as caught by Father's camera, long ago, from the helicopter. Only Father emerging sane from the harrowing flight. The lapis lazuli, if solid, the greatest treasure on Earth outside ancient Ur of the Chaldees. Actually not solid. Not lapis lazuli either. Actually a mishap in the laboratory in the third year of Father's science degree following upon the Second World War, when he was ex air force, free, with living allowance. Giving attention to engineering and architecture, too; six years in all; all with living allowance and free.

Hence, in due course, for monumental year upon year, everyone except the local Guild of Architects raving about this realisation of the fundamental mass, this return to the ziggurat, as conceived by the genius of Canute. Even the Brits, grudgingly, acknowledged it was there.

'His knighthood is but a matter of time,' was the opinion among the elderly and infirm jostling past the front gate in their wheelchairs of a Sunday morning. 'It'll be good for the neighbourhood to have a knight at the crossroads on the way to church. Since the death of our dear Sir Roscoe, the district hasn't been the same; no knight down the street to add class to our name.'

'Father,' said Knut. 'Would you really accept a knighthood like a common subject of the British Queen?'

'Of course I bloody would. Wouldn't you?'

'I imagine, sir, that coming second in a class of nineteen isn't the stuff that puts me near the head of the queue.'

Father was withholding the information that he had been thirty-second in a class of forty-eight.

'Perhaps,' said the spirits in transit, 'as Sir Richard, he could be encouraged to attend church at Christmas and Easter. And marry the lady. If only someone could discourage her from writing those grubby little books.'

'High time,' the Sunday press went on saying of the ziggurat, 'that we saw more of this movement away from shimmering boxes of glass. With each new concept Canute strikes a blow against monstrosities stuck together with plastics. What happens when the sticky stuff fails? The ozone layer. The European wasp. The termite. Who needs the bomb? We have adhesives with a use-by date.'

Yet Father went on living in sin in his little wooden box with the slate roof and the shingles and the ridges and the wrought-iron lace and the taxi cab on blocks. Along with the inspirational sun-bleached plaster gnome in the coy plaster cap beside the leaking goldfish pond that Father topped up, if at home, each Sunday morning at 10.55, except when gentle rain fell from Heaven. Sadly, no fish. Not seen in years. Just waterlilies, water snails, mosquito larvae, tadpoles and the attentions of the devoted kookaburras in the upper branches of *Eucalyptus ficifolia*.

But then came the sirens to startle Knut, and the flashing lights and the Billingsgate-type shouts which declined to go away. Troubled and exhausted sleep might have scored a further punch or two; but uproar won the fight.

'Damn!' Coming from Knut with passion. 'It's a filthy plot to drag me out of bed.'

Worming from beneath his doona. Moving to the edge into a shock of cold. The room was so oddly dark. What of the flashing lights below? Where had they gone? And what of the window glow, the sirens, and the shouts? Curiously and suddenly, no light and no sound.

Knut was shivering, disoriented, seeking to settle his feet in his slippers, not even knowing where the window lay. No clue of any kind. Stretching to locate the curtains. Not to be found. Groping for the light switch which usually came on at once under his hand. Nothing was where it should have been.

'The power's off! But how can it be? With the clock still showing at 1.17?'

Knut, making a try for the door, instantly detected another irregularity.

'I'm naked!'

Fright now, of a deep and penetrating kind, with Knut on his feet, swaying.

'Everything's wrong! Good God, have I died? Am I dead?'

Shrieking, *'My darling, darling Nanette! What do I do?'*

The voice of a woman said, 'Be calm. Be still.'

'Have I gone? Why have I gone? Why am I dead?'

The voice said, 'Be calm. Be still.'

'Why, for God's sake? I'm only seventeen. Seventeen!'

Knut on his feet. Swaying. Losing balance. Falling into a stretched instant, there just short of meeting, possibly, the sharp edge of his lovely sound-proofed door constructed by himself. A door thought to be shut, as it almost always was.

In this same stretched instant, this very instant, many of the issues here documented, along with others from his earliest memories through to Father, to Mother, to a life compressed, and to his despair for Nanette, were allowed entry and given time to file past. A moment as remarkable as any in the course of his life, except for his splendid birth.

This was an instant long enough, it seems, for all things to move, for all things to stop, for all things to readjust, for all things to be or not to be, though precisely what in all respects may for ever remain the question.

FACES IN THE CROWD

*In which are chronicled several
matters critically related to
dimension.*

The condition of Knut's room at the head of the stairs failed to
yield proof that violence had occurred. Of his departure no evidence was obvious other than his absence. The door to his room
was found closed, as usual. Also closed, indeed locked, was the
door adjacent to the foot of the stairs, affording access to the
back porch, the compost pit, the drying line and the hot tub, as
well as providing Knut's own exit to the outside world.

Not to suggest that Knut actually approached this porch in
the early hours of July 4. There were fragments of memory in
the minds of neighbours that the uproar in Sebastian Street
wasn't heard at any distance of consequence. As if a storm cloud
had snagged on an obstacle halfway across the street, drowning
everything else out. No Billingsgate fishwife, for instance, was to
be heard in any adjoining backyard corrupting the winter pars-
ley or the garlic chives. But a smell was in the air, some said, like
the burning of fabric, hair, or hide.

And why the pulsing glow, like a life force made visible, sufficient to infuse the stark branches of nearby deciduous trees?
Even appearing to regenerate the dead Judas tree on the Canute

fenceline to Johann Street. No mention of this phenomenon appears in any official reconstruction of the scene.

One must give some thought to the age and reliability of memory of several principal witnesses, 'old buggerlugs' from next door among them and very greatly distressed.

Equally puzzling were aspects of the accident itself. Despite the commotion, injuries were slight. Both vehicles came to rest where the classic fire hydrant used to be; hence a geyser at once erupted from their midst. The drivers involved were stubbornly agreed that they had swerved to avoid a smoking black hole. Nearby residents, called as witnesses, firmly stated (despite their age) that only the roundabout and the black locust tree at its centre were there.

'We dodged the hole,' the drivers swore. 'We thought it was a gas main. We hit the fire hydrant instead. It was very bloody strange.'

Blood alcohol content in each case was of slight interest in the early stages of the enquiry.

It may not be irrelevant to observe that the accident would have held attention away from anything else occurring near the corner of Sebastian and Johann at the same time. Though obvious, this likelihood intrigued and troubled the members of the enquiry. The drivers of the two vehicles were not charged.

THE ISSUE OF
SELF-DEFENCE

Given the opportunity, could
Knut have made a fight of it?

So began the cosmic adventures of Knut Mannerheim Canute on
July 4 of that year.

July 4. Celebrated by a great nation as Independence Day,
though far, far to the south and west in one small community,
from time to time it was remembered as the day when the lights
went out at the corner of Sebastian and Johann Streets. Knut
was then aged seventeen years, three months and a day or two.
A day and an age most curious in some respects, as investigators
have observed.

The profoundly historic metaphor of the ball and chain at
once suggests itself. It arises from the critical precedent of 'Curly'
Canute, cheeky and impertinent young villain, sentenced on July
4, 1833, for thirty years by transportation to New South Wales
for robbing a coach driver on the Great North Road of eighteen
pence and of relieving, with boorish disrespect, an unnamed
high-born lady of her white gold brooch with pearls, but recently
delivered to her hand by Mr Nigel Forsythe Jnr of Fotheringill &
Forsythe, York. It was a transportation that plucked this
renegade Canute out of one desperate world and consigned him

to another. And from the seed of his loins, in the strangeness of time, sprang the germ of Christian Canute, bootmaker; from whose loins sprang Cameron Canute, clergyman; from whose loins sprang Richard Canute, engineer and architect; from whose loins in a fullness of years, sprang Knut Canute.

Some have asked whether this young man might have averted his fate – whatever its form – if a weapon had been at hand, close enough to make a threat of it. If one is required to protect one's life, even a household knife or a razor will do!

But nothing indicated that Knut had resisted. Razors ranked low on his list, anyway. A vigorous rub with a rough towel sufficing for a long weekend. Along with knighthoods, razors interested him but little until, in his sixteenth year, the pink thing with forget-me-nots on the stem came to his hand . . .

'Mother, if ladies own razors, why?'

'I know nothing of razors or of ladies. Ask Father.'

'Father has an electric whirligig. Black. Made in Zgerrmanee.'

'I have reports of it. I recall paying the bill.'

'Then whose razor is the pink one with the blade and the forget-me-nots on the stem?'

'There could be nothing so vulgar in this house.'

'Mother, I have news for you.'

'If so, what have you been doing in my bathroom?'

'In search, Mother dear, of the hair conditioner with secret ingredients. You know what a mess I look if I can't brush my hair down. Am I to blame myself for inherited faults? Who's responsible for what I am?'

'Ask Father. *His* family history is sufficiently blood-curdling.'

'Mother, well-supported theories suggest that the most influential gene pool lies within the female line.'

'Try telling that to my father.'

'He's dead.'

'I'll never forget the day. Poor Mother in her rocking-chair, tears studding the deep lines of her cheeks, knitting him a new pair of socks. She'd knitted hundreds before. She cried, "He'll wear them, I declare, in the box. It's bound to be bitterly cold out there."'

'Mother, prior to the death of Grandfather, your mother dropped dead on the Matterhorn when the rope broke.'

'That's incidental.'

'In the company of an *unnamed* gentleman.'

'I deny it.'

'Suspected to be . . . '

'Not another word out of you, wretched boy!'

'During your father's absence, Mother, on a raft drifting to Easter Island with what's-her-name.'

'That's gross, impertinent and unfounded.'

'I have it on the authority of Aunt Sophie.'

'Scandal-mongering old witch.'

More must be said. The truth aborts the question. Knut was not unarmed, not defenceless and not without skills to defend himself. Above his bed, within reach of his hand, was his rapier, an expensive souvenir given by Mother to celebrate the fact and the achievement: Knut Canute, National Champion, Intermediate Foil.

STOREHOUSE OF
NATIONAL TREASURES

*Knut reviews his life and times
and suspects that each has taken
a curious turn.*

Knut, low on high spirits, addressed the Universe on the occasion of beginning his great journey, his extraordinary adventure . . .

'This late-night bulletin is brought to you by Canute Incorporated, your former friendly storehouse of national treasures at the corner of Sebastian and Johann; Richard, Madeleine, and me.

'The news. You'll be charmed, I'm sure. It's taken a plunge for the abominably bad. Little doubt you demons at the bottom of the garden will be clapping your claws, but sit tight on your unsavoury salutations. I may not be as dead as formerly supposed.

'Life may not be extinct in my sacred structure. I'm conscious. I'm *here*. There must be something of me. So raspberry blurt-cakes to you lesser demons and deities of ill will. Squeeze, tail-first, back into your disgusting little bottles.

'God knows the truth, anyway, and He's out there somewhere knowing it. Which must be a great comfort to Him.'

This outbreak gave way to anxious contrition that might have lasted a week or two, during which Knut framed the statement: 'Perhaps some kindly seraph will advise interested parties around Latitude 38 South, Planet Earth, of an encouraging sign that death may not be permanent. You, of course, are well aware of the truth, though for us mortals, stressed by mortality, fighting to remain in touch with the magic flame, the issue invites endless argument.

'I suspect these reflections echo parental discussions over highly spiced dinners on late summer evenings and may be the last spasms of my grievously wounded body and brain.'

At another time Knut set out to say to the same audience, 'For instance . . . ' But at once sought safety in silence. At a much later date adding: 'I must not submit to the possibilities of a single "for instance". Only the Devil knows what it may stir up and one must suppose that only the One Great God knows what the Devil is.

'Believe me, you astral bodies, despite appearances, a number of indiscreet utterances recently made in our hearing could not have come from me. No doubt millions of self-opinionated young guys like me are wandering around out here among the stars making a big noise.'

Knut collected himself during the passing of another week or two.

'Right. Let's not consider the pain in my brain or the blood-like substance continually received from my brow into my left hand, though consideration may be prudent.

'Could this poor, injured thing be *me*? Is poor Knut holding in poor Knut's hand the last drops of his personal sticky stuff? Has his magical compound broken down? What of my darling

Nanette and her alluring possibilities? Is she to fill only a line in the book of life?'

Knut briefly seeking solace in silence. Breaking it: 'I pray it may be a trick of the red end of the spectrum, this pool of blood, though I could have sworn it was dead of night, pitch dark and just past 1.17 a.m.'

Substantially later, addressing the One Great God, Knut said: 'Sire, due to my state of nerves or to another of Your only knowings, the chill around here suggests that at bedtime I forgot to put my pyjamas on.

'My goodness, that Universe out there. All that immensity of time. All those planets whizzing around all those suns. All those galaxies clanking by like all those vehicles at my own little crossroads. How many vehicles? Don't challenge me, Sire. But square the number. Quadruple it. Compound it to the tenth. Stick it in the centrifuge. Press the button. Now, how many galaxies are there away out there in support of how many microscopic quantities of interstellar dust a little self-important like me? Or is the answer less complicated? Is it all arranged with mirrors? What sort of Universe am I in?

'Which leads me to wonder whether my sins of omission and commission have already invited Your severe correction?

'Nudity.

'There's little doubt I encounter Knut in the raw wherever I put a paw. Not red raw, mark you; it's blue cold out here. Or is the raw condition of my sacred body due to the central heat? The people downstairs in my house maintaining that hot air rises until my ceiling prevents its escape. They tell me that all the heat of the house mounts the stairs to my den, declining to make its way down again even for meals. Rubbish.

'Are not my manly muscles savaged with disfiguring goose pimples? Presenting the peppered aspect of the rough-plucked gander? And is not mid-winter the festive season for central heat? Away it goes, ducking out the back door, arm in arm with the hot-water service, heading for the bright lights, leaving us at the corner to get on with entertaining the cold. The evidence suggests I forgot to put my pyjamas on. And thus to the leading question? Why would I leave them off? God! If Nanette is not at home in her own bed, retribution must be at the door with the key in Mother's hand.

'Nanette! Wake up! The stupid clock let us down!'

'Correction. Correction! I recall the kissing of my sheet and at an earlier hour, the kissing of many squared centimetres along the street, even under the light at the corner of Johann and Crete. I hear again the voice: "Disgusting drunken lout. I'll call the police."

'I hear again my reply. "Drunk from none but love, ma'am. I kiss where her feet have trod."

'"If my love kissed my footsteps, I'd have him seen to."

'Well, for what reason but insanity would I take to my bed improperly dressed? Could I forget to put my pyjamas on? Do I forget to take them off? They're a reflex condition. Not the subject of classroom or parliamentary debate. On they go or off they come, depending upon the hour, the need, or whether they've been savaged on the ironing board or starched.

'Mother and I have an understanding about the undressed condition.

'In the hot flushes of my boyhood; she, at her whim, bursting into the bathroom for her hair conditioner, face washer, or the

62

ill-mannered delivery of some indecency: "Your knees. Your ears. Your fingernails. Your feet. Your operational zones. Scrub! Why is that object in that condition?"

'No beg pardons. No please, sweet child of mine, I apologise, I see you're not dressed to receive guests.

'I, having no reciprocal rights. Even when knocking politely and knowing there'd be little worth viewing except a ruff of bubbles about her neck.

'Tap-tapping the little knocker of the lady stepping into her bath.

'Mummay. It is I. Your honey-bunnay. Your Knut. May I come in?

'"You may not. Go read your story books. They're dedicated to you, as everybody knows but you. Refer to page v. Familiarise yourself with the author's name. It may be required when you fill in your marriage certificate."

'Oh, please, Mummay. I have a secret to share.

'"Share it with the lady next door."

'She's too old.

'"So am I."

'Enchanting Nanette would kill me for forgetting to put my pyjamas on. Well, I trust she would.

'Why, enchanting Nanette, in my condition of undress, in the presence of an unknown lady, are you not knifing me repeatedly to death?'

'Any suggestion that death has already occurred and that nudity is less than a mere figure of speech would not excite my respect. Nanette must not be told that I find myself reclining upon the floor in a historic fashion, arrayed in my splendour of skin as if upon one of those couch things, as if attended by hound dogs, gorgeous goblets of wine and dancing girls in natural neck-to-ankle costume.'

Knut was becoming insecure.

Were the universal powers noting these utterances? Were they held enthralled by his late-night bulletin? Were there clearings of the throat out there in deep space? Better if they'd send him a pair of jockeys.

Hark, thought Knut. What's that I hear?

'Tell us more, lovely lad. You excite the eternal thirst for the new heresy. You get each of us, the All and the One, on the buzz again.'

'Well,' said Knut modestly, 'well, well! I was under a spot of pressure at bedtime. Actually, about a tonne of it for reasons related to the imminent return of aged parents and several urgent procedures of personal hygiene, good housekeeping and the covering-up of one's tracks. Even on Earth one is not obligated to incriminate oneself. Which places the procedures beyond the discipline of the universal bureaucracies. But I swear no person was in my room at the time and no lady was among them, which is more than can be said now.'

Knut was banging his fist emphatically upon something or other and concentrating upon the lady he could hear addressing him.

'Uninvited lady. I suggest no cultured person, fully dressed, would embarrass me thus, except Mother dear. True, you remind me of that portrait of Grandmother by what's-his-name. Also true, you glow like an icon with holy fires within. Which, in Grandmother's case, would be nonsense. Probably in your case, too.

'We were reading the late-night news, I believe, as addressed to the Universe. Now which calamity was occupying our attention? Sirens, strobes and the thunderous assault of storms against windowpanes! Along with the expectations of eager little men with axe blades finally cracking our zero per cent on fire brigades!

'Where is this fire, anyway? Downstairs? In the roof? Here, there, anywhere at all? Raging through the property next door? Now *there's* an appropriate address. Not that I wish old buggerlugs any further disfigurement, but he's grizzled and worn and dog-eared and torn. As for me, I've scarcely whetted my appetites.

'It makes sense, all round, that old buggerlugs should be enjoying the flames. I can't see myself making a good fire. I haven't had time to generate the fat or the sins.

'It's good to observe no fiery tongues licking my wall and no smoke at hand. Nor do I hear the flashing axe blades at the entry. Or glimpse the heat-flushed cheeks and brass-bright helmets and red-rimmed eyes of the fearless firefighters confronting their first conflagration in forty years.

'Or is it, madam, like some dizzy dame, you're lit up on the phosphorus at cocktail time?

'You could have had a sly dry ginger. No reasonable host refuses a guest pleading from the knees. Ask, also, for a slice of lemon on the edge of the glass. And the temperance union delegate stuck to the ceiling, disguised as a huntsman spider, will file your name as shameless and drunken along with the rest, thus satisfying honour. It's me favourite ploy, madam, in social situations getting out of hand. Thus, to the very end, you remain able to respond even if addressed upon entry: "Honey-bunny.

Breathe upon me. Let me catch the stupefying drift of your breath."

'A breath, madam, as sweet as the lily of the lea. On your way out shut the door, please.

'Do I truly present a regimentally improper aspect? A likeness, begging his pardon, of the respected parent caught short? When I had my appendix out I wore a gown up front. Prim and appropriate, I thought. An appealing character sketch. Though I recollect a breeze striking me from astern causing minor concern, for bringing up the rear was this little Nightingale aged seventeen. I, at the time, a year short of that, but a hundred and eighty-six centimetres tall, ten centimetres chest expansion and numerous other features I'm too modest to define. What *was* my little Nightingale doing back there, bringing up the rear? I thought student nurses were not given to curiosity of that kind.'

On another occasion, Knut might have said:

'Madam, I will not go down the stairs. I insist. You may perform like a picture with its face to the wall, but I decline to descend the stairs whether fire threatens, or earthquake, or nothing threatens but your own stolid exterior. Have you not observed that I'm bleeding to death? My little Nightingale would've leapt to my aid with bandages and medicaments and gently invasive hands. Was she not leaping in my direction continually?

'You're nothing but a common nag, madam. Deafening me with your implacable silence. Reminding me strongly of the Grandmother Mannerheim portrait in Mother's writing-room. Go suck an egg. Preferably hard boiled a la Madeleine. Under which the gas, as usual, has failed to ignite. Why should I, along with my male parent, suffer egg nogs ad infinitum, from methods learned, no doubt, at your never-bending knee? There's bound to be a nice sloshy one in wait downstairs. Go, feast upon it. Inhale deeply while you're there. Strike the match to confirm that you've arrived at the correct saucepan; *per ardua ad astra*, through difficulties to the stars, or something of the kind. After all, the valiant few is at hand, with their fire axes and brass helmets, knocking on doors. "Who's hiding our conflagration? Who's sitting on our fire? Here we are out of bed in the middle of the night, fine tuned, dead keen, pumps pumping, hoses gushing, foam foaming, and not a flame to be seen. That's a nice little heap of waste paper you have there, lad!"

'Sir. That's no heap of waste paper. That's my mother's next book.'

'Allow us, please. Stand aside while we sluice it with a slosh or two of kerosene.'

'Alternatively, madam, one step closer and I'll bite your kneecap. I have teeth like a sabre-toothed tiger. Aged eleven I severed a walnut in the shell at a single bite. Then we'll find who's dead and who's alive, won't we? The orthodontist did handsomely, I recall. He donated to the town square a statue of the walnut extruding one front tooth. You might well turn out, shortly, to be severed in like manner. With *two* teeth extruding, one a crown bearing the signature of the orthodontist.

'What's that, you say? You must speak louder. Your voice, madam, I cannot hear. You're a demon. God forbid, a Cootamundra Wattle Gnome.

'Hour by hour, these past years, I've been dreading an encounter with one of your kind. Creeping under the door. Coming up through the floor. Mother's fault. Ridiculous blaming Father at his age!'

Later, Knut may have said: 'If you threaten me with a meat cleaver illegally removed from Mother's kitchen, I may ignore you. Indeed, I may decline to speak with you. I may withdraw to meditate. Then where will you be? All lit up like a runway and not a serviceable aircraft in sight.

'Speaking for myself, and I'm the crux of the issue, the son and heir, the "I am", the crown prince – and modest at that. All that's accomplished at this address is in my name unless I predecease them. An obscene idea.

'How can I keep to the point of the argument, madam, if you stubbornly refuse to interrupt?'

He knew it had to be *her*, his grandmother, though she had fallen to her death on the Matterhorn before he was born.

Or did that realisation come later when he feared he was within a breath or two of bleeding to death? Interesting him intensely.

So it was that Knut was trying to relate these various dimensions one to the other, and was asking questions: 'What time and place is this? Where can I be? Why am I in darkness? Why can't I see myself as I see her, glowing like an icon alone in a great depth out of reach?'

CHAPTER
TWELVE

TIME AND THE
SACRED STRUCTURE

*Knut stresses his innocence
and asks why he should be
abandoned or slain.*

At the conclusion of these former meditations, in a darkness without presences and in an immensity where he was little more than an awareness of himself, Knut asked, 'Can this poor shell be me?'

His question came in the shape of a cry, as an entry in a timid hand in the ancient diary he kept in his head.

'It has worsened by the hour,' he said, even hearing his own voice from a great distance. 'By the hours, days and weeks that have passed. It's alien here. As if silences and stillnesses were consuming me. Were changing me into something I refuse to be.

'I will not lie like a dead bird beside the road. I am Knut. Does the bird declare the same?

'I struggle with the idea of nothing. No mate beside me to shelter me with wings. As if I had never been loved by those beautiful people of mine.

'What harm have I done to anyone I know or to millions whose names I have never heard? If I've inflicted harm, I didn't know. They tell me the law does not let you go, whether you know – or not.

'The work of my life was to grow where I was put. It was not my fault they were not drunken or brutal or warped. Could I have chosen Richard and Madeleine? Could such a little thing have been so wise?

'Why do I feel myself draining, draining, draining into my cupped hand? Why should there be a messy end to all those perfect days? Was it only a door into which I walked? How could my heart have failed at seventeen? What pain have I ever felt? An appendix. A rogue tooth. A wound of pride. The strike of the foil to my cheek.

'Have I been slain in my bed like the crown prince?

'Could Knut Canute by birth have earned that kind of fate?

'Was I murdered? Was I mistaken for Father? But Father doesn't press the button. Doesn't need minders. Father lives in a little house at the corner of Sebastian and Johann, even though the world knows his name. Who gets murdered for being a genius at his kind of game?

'Or, is this the cutting edge of an ancient wound? Did it happen to me back among the dinosaurs? Did it come down to me through my genes? Has my life been nothing more than the dream of someone who lived in a much earlier time?

'Might a gnarled club, way back then, have taken me by surprise? Five thousand, ten thousand, twenty thousand years gone? Was I sacrificed to some tribal god with a thirst for blood? Was it a spear, a lance, an arrow or a two-handed sword? Was it a dumdum bullet on the Somme? A cannon shell in 1940? Was my Hurricane or Messerschmitt the flame that ignited my funeral pyre? And now, now, now, am I twenty thousand years down the line?

'Why would anyone do this to me and not explain? I'm the

70

reason for everything that made me. There's no Canute or Mannerheim to come after me. I'm the end of the line.

'Or might it have been a fire so hot that God made sure I wouldn't remember or feel it? I have often wondered whether mercies of that kind have been arranged?'

A great time later . . .

Into the same darkness, the same silence, the same emptiness, Knut said: 'Mother . . . are you so wrapped in the new book that you haven't heard my call? I might have been calling you for years. I begin to wonder if I made you up?

'Father. I declare I've never spoken of you bitterly, disrespectfully or mockingly. With confusion a few times and anxiously often. But I've loved you and honoured you. Why haven't you come? Do other interests outrank me? Like supper at Susannah's to celebrate the night I was supposedly conceived?

'Aunt Sophie. Aunt Ingrid. From the pictures in my heart, I know you've not stopped caring.

'Cousin Jacqueline. Dear Jacqueline. Was it a week or a month or a year that we last held hands and cried?

'Cousin Claus. Our bike rides. Our smiles along the roads. Our climbing of trees. Our sharing of boughs. Our delight in the blood of the family. "I could have been you," you said. "And I you," said I.

'It was a pine tree. About forty feet up.

'"Would you rather," you said, "have been me?"

'"Oh, Claus, no," said I, "for then I wouldn't have seen you as I see you now. I'd have looked in a mirror at me."

'Harcourt. Down the street on the other side. Half a dozen doors away. Number fifty-three. When you went away, I thought

I'd die. You were six. So was I. If you come, if you can, if you remember me, take care. Doors have edges. Kitchens have cleavers. Gardens have guns. I don't know about bombs and beds.

'Robert. Grade Eight. Grade Nine. Grade Ten. We were born on the same day. We'll be there, we said, 2020, under the great clock of Father's ziggurat, even if we come from opposite ends of the Earth. April 1. Twelve noon. Only Doomsday, we said, can bring it on sooner. Robert; I'm calling. Doomsday has come.

'Nanette. My darling. My dear heart. My only one since I was twelve, though I had not seen you then. Your silence is a cold room of grey stone. Everyone in the world has gone home, except for that little thing out in the middle, in a huddle, that used to be me. Why, enchanting friend, have you made this tomb for me, to share with the spectre of *Bill* – who had no substance before your mother's silly joke or her slip of the tongue?

'Why have the people I love abandoned me?'

'What is this place where nothing can be seen or heard? Where nothing is. By what train did I arrive? Upon what plane or ship? Did I buy a ticket? Did I stow away?

'Where has the blood gone from my hands? Hey?

'What is this scene of emptiness?

'I'm intrigued that I'm brave enough to raise the issue, for I fear every answer but the one I'm unlikely to receive: Sleep on, honey-bunny. Soon it'll be morning and time for soggy corn-flakes and a stone cold egg.

'Now, if I'm dead, wouldn't someone be helping me across the great river? Of all the people through all the thousands of years, their seed in me, making me, coming all the way down to me, all that suffering and magic and love, why hasn't anyone come?'

CHAPTER
THIRTEEN

WEDNESDAY TO TUESDAY 1.17A.M. INCLUSIVE

A review of the week of
The Turn of the Screw.

Knut said, 'Everything in my head hurts so bloody much. And everything's so bloody dark. But why am I seeing rainbows? Are they in my stupid head? There's a skyline. But it's dark.

'Am I in a Jumbo at 40,000 feet?

'Have I become like Father? Am I taking a flight home?

'Am I unexpected? Am I knocking at the door at the corner of Sebastian and Johann?

'God; wouldn't it be bloody marvellous.'

Yes. The Wednesday evening of June 28 when Mother said: 'Do you hear? Do you hear? It's his knock.'

Mother rushing to the door.

'Oh, my God. Don't tell me you're dead. I'm in bed. It's a nightmare. Oh, my God.'

'I can't find my small change,' Father said. 'I require fifty negotiable dollars for the taxi driver.'

Mother dancing on the doorstep. 'You're back. Oh, you're back. You didn't let me know, you fiend! But you couldn't, you wouldn't dare to have eaten a bite. Would you?'

'Nothing, dear heart, but supper, breakfast, morning coffee, lunch, afternoon tea, a couple of bottles of red and a modest cognac or two. Fifty dollars, if you don't mind. If you're really over the moon, make it sixty, and we'll send him off happy.'

Mother was excelling in the kitchen with blood-boiling flavours barely on the survival side of brutal, adding the diversion of a blousy gown thrown on with resourceful carelessness.

It was not the house for a hearty male to abandon, gourmet or gallant, except in the event of fire or structural failure in adjoining rooms.

'The Pacific,' Father said at a high point of the evening, 'forty thousand feet, I'd say. Tail wind like a tempest. Clouds like islands touched with fire and ice . . .

'Well, you give of your best for a lifetime and hear third, fourth, fifth hand (was it only Monday?) around level sixty-three, from a guy washing his paws in a plasterer's bucket full of corporation blood that the job's gone bust and the bastards owe him five weeks' pay. God Almighty, what of the architect? What do they owe *me*?'

Father grabbing for gulps of air.

'Far below, family, from my rough-cut business-class accommodation, I espied this sea that might be described as frozen rose-pink. No sun. Not a stray ray. For hours, like a fat old duck with a gammy leg, the sun mucking around on the other side of the fence. Playing with whom? The moon? Or its reflection? The solemn truth, I swear.'

'Father . . . What fence?'

'You're a changeling.'

'Well, you'd know, sir.'

'The fence of mirrors at the edge of the world! What else? High time for the sun to be showing its hand. A feeling confirmed by my old timepiece, my Jaeger-LeCoultre watch, for which I tendered funds in Zurich an age before your mother seduced me and I became enfeebled by non-portable effects. I ask, was the sun snagged on some riotous rosebush at the edge of Heaven that some beastly little saint, corruptly canonised for chastity, obedience and poverty had failed to cut back?'

Father added after a dominant pause that would have savaged the most adroit interjector: 'Pleasant metaphors, the rosebush, the fence of mirrors, the edge of Heaven, the recalcitrant saint. But I don't believe in "other-worldly" experience. I don't collect absurdities. But I do confirm the fence and the reflections! In a coldly distant frame of mind, I photographed what my puny eyes perceived, remarking to Command, "None of it's there. I'm calling Your bluff, Mate!"'

'Command, sir?'

'The Godhead, blockhead!'

Father was drumming multiple fingertips along the table edge. 'These shots can't come out.'

Mother said: 'You took them.'

Father said: 'Save your flatteries, madam, for those in need of them! His hands were tied. Could He fiddle the fundamentals of physics to humour a bum like me? *Not even I may photograph the ill-tempered illusions of a wounded ego.* Cameras don't see subjectively. The lens is a predictable device or there'd be no family album of nativities, visits to the zoo or bunfights on birthdays. A "trick" of the camera is a technical conundrum having bugger all to do with the postures of a wounded psyche.'

...

75

FRIDAY: Father is at his work table in the small conservatory on the north side of the house, framed by orchids, African violets, cacti and map drawers bulging with dreams. Chin on thumb, cheekbone on forefinger (shades of portrait, 1971), duty-free cognac at elbow, he is brooding over the shots that couldn't come out. But had.

'I don't believe it, Knut. It's a hiccup.

'I hear the voice of Command addressing me and I wish He were not: *A few miserable years, Richard, posturing on girders, making an exhibition of yourself, disfiguring natural materials that've taken Me for ever to accomplish and I hear your whinings over a mere percentage? If you doubled your losses for famine relief you wouldn't feel it. Give a thought to My "for ever" and the persistent insensitivity of your genus. Give a thought to the dear departed, full of virtue, though in life full of lust, avarice and kindness. Give a thought to those presently with us, if you're strong enough. Give no thought, for fear of cardiac arrest, to those about to be conceived by chance or intent. Where, Richard, away from your drawing board, is your sense of perspective?*

'If I had a wooden leg,' Father said, 'I'd thump it out of embarrassment.'

SUNDAY: A minute to eight a.m. Father walking in on St Sebastian's.

Over brunch addressing himself, but from time to time counting in Mother and possibly Knut.

'Thirty-three years since my last encounter with a holy interior. I'm not much given to attending weddings or funerals as you know.

'The wheelchair set made me most welcome, considering my publicised decadence of the last half-century which must've stressed their envy.

'How could I mouth repentance? What an appendage to the delights of a thousand and one nights. Though I submit it was of interest to feel a twinge. Arthritis, I imagine. It's cold on the tiles at my age.

'But I was dipping my lid to the great originator. A private matter. I valued your support, Madeleine. You were the red rose in my lapel. For you, Knut, a reproof! I refer to the elderly popinjay who sports the cane that twirls as it passes my gate.'

'Yes, sir?'

'None but he trekked with Alaskan Malamutes and Siberian Samoyeds to the pole when I was but a brash youth. And he never got bloody knighted for it, either.'

'Yes, sir.'

'You know he lives within gunshot?'

'Of course, sir.'

'Are you my liaison officer?'

'Proudly, sir.'

'You've failed me.'

'Never, sir.'

'You mean yes, sir.'

'Never, sir. I've been telling you repeatedly. I've heard Mother backing me up.'

'I could've shaken that *marvellous* human being by the hand. Damn it, we could've been confederates through all these years. What an abominable son.'

Knut was glowing in the glory.

...

MONDAY: *The Turn of the Screw*, in parallel with the image, the wonder and the fragility of Nanette De L'isle.

TUESDAY AT 1.17 A.M.: Curtain.

Never was Knut to come back to knock at the door as his father had done. With each moment, through each instant in his strange cocoon, he drew farther away.

Drew farther and farther distant from Earth's calendar, Earth's clock and Earth's open door, where the past grew longer day by day.

And drew closer and closer to a place where the present was continuous and the past was somewhere else.

PART TWO
THE ADAM
BOMB

THE SNAKE PIT

Knut argues that wickedness
is an essential component of
happiness.

Thus Knut was obliged to go on through an unknown time never to be measured by clocks, calendars or kilometres, before he dared to grasp at his sacred head: before he dared to hold between his hands what life or death had made of him; to know what mischief or murder had been done upon him.

'I have in my head,' Knut said, 'if I have a head, the kind of puzzle I find in late-night readings of Father's library books; the puzzle dropped on the desk of the smart guy at MI5. Items of information without visible connection. That's the way it is.

'The smart guy knows that these items fit together, that the connection is there or none of it would be on his desk. Just as I know there's a connection or I wouldn't be battling with the idea.

'The smart guy will be long in the tooth or bright-eyed and bushy-tailed. Some say only the old are wise enough to solve the puzzle. Others know that only the young are strong enough to try. People in the middle, Father says, rarely solve problems; they manufacture them; then sink in the midst of them.

'It could be that this puzzle was meant for Father, but he's not dealing with it. Maybe he was the target, but the young guy was lying vulnerable upstairs, nursing the wreckage of his love dreams. Me . . . '

Knut's head started hurting so much he could not proceed, but was reassured by a strong feeling that it was not expected of him.

Later he said: 'If I really am left with half a head, am I left with half a brain? Two sides, they tell me. Two rooms. The side for realities. The side for illusions. How do the experts read the nameplates on the doors? The side for the reckless as opposed to the timid. The fearful side fighting it out with the brave. The good and the bad at war.

'This must be why everyone I know is such a mess.

'Bet your life it's my wicked half that's dropped off behind, taking the entertainment industry with it. And it was due for a fling, poor thing. So it's what's left that worries me. Am I in danger of being stuck with all my virtue without any comic relief? Of being left with the side where the lip goes down? Where everything has to be thought through. That breaks out in a rash under questioning and tosses the hair down over the scar on the cheek. My badge of honour, I say, from falling upstairs fleeing from Mother. Broom handle out in front looking lethal. Woman with broom being a dangerous animal. Well, it's the story that gets the laugh. But in truth a mishap, acquired in defence of my National Championship, Intermediate Foil. I reckoned I'd be blind at least.

'So I hope you minor gods, or whatever you are, in charge of wherever I am, are on radio watch, receiving my application for a whole head. On moral grounds you can hardly lumber me with the virtuous half I've been living with for so long; costing me the pleasures that other guys take for granted. Who in the real world believes I'm as pure as the lily? Does Mother? Does my darling? I'll bet not Father.

'What happens when finally I fine-tune for mortal combat? When I go for the big settlement with the human race? My darling Nanette gets cold feet. I ought to bloody shoot myself. If someone like her father hasn't shot me already! (Which is an unappealing thought I could have done without.)

'I require my wicked inner self to be given some freedom; where did it come from if it's not in the genes? And on aesthetic grounds, along with the moral ones, you can't have me disfiguring the landscape with half a head. And give a thought to the legion of gorgeous girls in whose company I have sublimated my natural chauvinism in expectation of a few favours later on.'

Knut at last sought to address the landscape he found himself in, his invisible landscape, this physical presence of a landscape submerged in darkness, the sensing of it, but receiving in no direct way a sight or a sound of it. Enduring only the depths of night as if they were to be everlasting.

'So what can be out there other than some common or garden landscape too modest or too cowardly or too mobile to show a face. It is in no way known to me, despite the likelihood that we have suffered each other's company for more than long enough already. I suggest that whatever you are was long ago determined and you might as well show yourself. Why go on hiding in the dark? Or is this world that we share so large that the sun comes up only once a week. Or have you taken a break? Are you on long-service leave?

'Landscapes, once established, are expected to remain in one place. They are not self-propelled. Ask Father. They don't rush about after dark. I stress, I did not bring my landscape with me. I had no time to pack. You were here before I got here. You are ancient, without a doubt, and I am but a youth.

'Again I stress, landscapes do not depart overnight or take possession of the street around the corner, thus to bring confusion upon property surveyors, town councillors, bus drivers, contract gardeners and abandoned young gentlemen with an unfulfilled flair for shy maids. Believe me, landscapes never earned a guernsey in my traffic survey. Not as Land Rover or Land Cruiser or landmine. Landscapes are not supposed to assume the properties of vehicles in motion. Which, I concede, might suggest that the party on the move continues to be me, still heading into eternal darkness, leaving my traffic survey still farther and farther behind.

'Take care, my friends, of what I have left back there. My landscape took a lifetime to put together.'

Now and then an outside voice stirred at the recurring pain in Knut's brain. It could not, he believed, be the local idea of muzak. It must have had something to do with the mechanics of pain.

On a less harrowing day he'd have thought of the voice as athletic; practiced rather than gifted. Even a crow on a telegraph pole or a monk striving for union with the Great Beyond. Perhaps a cosmic replay of a tune hummed by a lady knitting socks at the foot of the guillotine. Interesting alternatives. Daunting.

Knut went wandering on among these choices until he

realised he was focussed on rainbows above illuminated mists. Nothing solid, but they were there. They were real. They were visible.

A view was opening up – as if seen from a mountain; as if from a cliff at the edge of a misted abyss. Rainbows and mist; nothing more. But not an eternal darkness to go on filling a grievously wounded head. How pleasant it would be if they stayed.

Please. Please.

They might not settle anything beyond doubt, clarify memories of any one scene, but they *did* agree with the idea that the world was an extension of himself, of his mood, as was Father's Pacific at 40,000 feet. Yet this was an awesomeness and a remoteness that could never have happened at home at the corner of Sebastian and Johann Streets. Perhaps Knut was seeing to the ends of the world and discovering new beginnings in himself . . .

'That's a thought,' he thought. 'I must hold to it. I must hold to it.'

Aloud he said, 'A mountain has been hiding in me.' But at once he became afraid and fell silent.

Later he managed to say, 'You never see your appendix until they take it out. You don't see it then, thank God. Might mountains and I have a lot in common?'

Long, long afterwards, he said firmly, aloud: 'I am determined not to go back to the mountain where those two people were busy making me. I'm too young, too silly, too scared and too small inside to become the mountain where I began. Any other mountain will do.'

Whereupon the strange song and the rainbows and the

landscape (whatever it might have been) melted into the enveloping mist and Knut went crawling into a tiny space where there were no sights or sounds or thinkings or feelings and it was possible to get along with the pain.

Now for the other face. The absurd. The wise live with life as if it were absurd. Once one sees the absurdity, even the dark and awful experiences may be survived with dignity and with flair.

Mother might have considered Knut to be a captive of the bad lads at the larrikin end of the cosmos; even of the infamous Wattle Gnomes of the books that had made her fame and assured her immortality while poets languished.

Knut, carried off by these hooligan creatures, through the dead hours of space and dumped in the palace of pleasures to recover unaided. While the Gnomes in their disguises, as trolls and demons and devils, peered through latticed screens over balconies, around the edges of improperly acquired Ming vases, waiting for Knut to make his break for freedom. It was a thought; indeed, it might have been more!

Were the nets about to fall? The trapdoors to open? Was he to be dropped into the lions' den, shot into the snake pit or fed directly to the kabana machine?

Mother would have said: Go out in style. But first take a look at the bars of your cage. Are they and the distances that isolate you made of the same stuff?

She'd have had a book about it on the way. Mother didn't fool around.

Page one: readers hardly out of their romper suits startled out of their disposable nappies; Knut getting fed to the kabana machine.

Page four: readers turning green. Knut's side-products draining off for the dragons, the health food companies, the alley cats and the stormwater drains.

Page seven: involuntary nerve-twitchings among the more robust tiny tots about the stage. Mother having a wonderful time in the wings, side-saddle on her broomstick, against the blood-stained moon. Knut on sale at the local dellie by the can, the carton, the measure or the slice, served with a bread roll.

'The absurd,' Knut said, 'makes real life endurable.'

So what *was* Knut's new landscape? A mountain side? A cliff face? The cutting edge of an abyss? Knut standing there. Might a rift valley have lain down there within the mist? Or a tableland? Or a vast river delta, in the style of the Ganges? Or a sea?

'I vote for the tableland,' Knut said, 'set for a banquet screened by a cloth of mist. Nothing left showing to excite the mischief of the media. No place at the table except by written invitation delivered by footmen; a hundred thousand footmen marching through the mist in line astern calling each guest by name.

'Dark deserts of mist out there. Pillars and domes of it surmounting crystal carafes of fine wine and silver salvers of roasted game – of limited appeal to us vegetarians. But passing beyond the horizon, out beneath the rainbows, more fine wines and gourmet dishes based on chilli and the soy bean. Excellent. Excellent. A hundred thousand diners reclining upon their decadent couch things raising their goblets to salute the arrival of the king. Poor bloody king.'

Repeatedly, the scene came back to mind. Which could have

implied that nothing new was happening out there. Yet Knut was aware that he, in person, appeared to be very, very small. If this experience, he thought, signals the end of the journey, have I arrived?

If I'm at the controls of this aircraft, I'd better get my undercart down! If I'm a traveller, a captive or a slave, where are my travelling companions? One doesn't achieve a passage of this kind alone.

Where are the aircrews? Where are the seamen, the coach driver, the railwaymen? Where is the QE2 or the train? Where are the longed-for faces of my family and friends in the waiting crowd? Where is my darling Nanette?

Knut looked farther and farther around. In one direction there was no skyline, no rainbows. The face of the mountain itself was vanishing in the mist. If he lost his grip he'd be falling for years into an abyss.

He was in fear now of the faintest move, taking care with his breath, wishing not to upset the balance between here and everywhere else. 'I have a question,' he said, far back inside where it raised no ripple in the material world. 'Does a human go on breathing when he's dead? Is there anything that can go on breathing with half a head? If I'm not dead, tell me how I got here?'

Had a threshold intervened? Had the hard edge of his attic door moved aside a little more and allowed him through? What of this surface upon which he barely stood; rather, to which he clung? Was it timber, rock, sand, snow, ice?

'I wonder if I really want to know.'

To which the Universe replied, 'Moral cowardice is not in the program.'

Knut cried, 'You don't care if there's only half of me.'

'Half of you or all of you; does it matter? All ways we win; all ways you lose, unless you grasp the key.'

Knut had known *that*, from the moment of 1.17 past midnight on July 4. Was it an hour ago, yesterday, or a geological age removed?

Who or what was to emerge from this trial? Or was it to be regarded as an execution without trial?

Might a young man emerge? Or a person very old by human measure? Might the body at the end prove to be a husk from which life had long been extinguished?

Or was Knut to emerge as he was, still at heart a boy? Many they were who hoped so.

What lay in wait for this greatly stressed young man?

Was the reality to prove, even yet, to be an event happening by chance in another dimension? Or was Knut, in some way, still lodged in the attic room at the head of the stairs; stamping ground of the boy; same address as the London cab on blocks, the hot tub and the traffic survey; scene of his one romantic endeavour; the brief physical, magical presence of his loved Nanette De L'isle?

No. Of all these alternatives, none.

SILENCE OF
VIOLENCE

*In which Knut discovers that
bone survives the flesh and
rainbows are dreams.*

Knut found himself wondering for a period whether the price of
life was to be reckoned in dead weight. Giving thought to the
idea that every tension pain of the past had turned into a cannon ball lodged under his ribs. No wonder, for there he sat, with
his hands held hard to his head.

There he sat with his elbows jammed into the cannon ball. With
arrowed aches like weapon strikes reaching even to the roots of
his teeth. Was it to be proved that only the young, the fit and the
hardy would have emerged with a tale to tell? Were others, of
an age like Father, to lie like birds at the roadside?
    Knut believed he was instructing his body to straighten, but
in the same instant became certain that protons and neutrons
and pistons in cylinders were charging through his veins as if he
were composed of living flesh and blood.

Knut started raising himself through an exquisitely strange
period of growth.

Here I am aged two months.

Here I am at six years.

Now, I am aged fourteen.

Here I am in splendour, reconstituted bone and dust, leaping back from several hundred years of sleep.

It was a stretching for the light like a germinating seed. Of fearing that his head might shoot so high that he'd fall back into the night and be lost again, for a time, unless his feet took root like cedars.

Knut upright, triumphantly, swaying as if buffeted by winds. In flat calm? Knowing that marvellous blood was coursing through him; yet might the blood be sap? Could he have become an oak, an elm, or a banyan tree?

Knut peered into his long, lean hands.

Not a root to be seen. Not a branch, twig, or leaf. Not a trace of blood in his palms.

Knut then caught sight of his sleeves!

The royal blue close-fitting sleeves of his pyjamas worn at bedtime, very late, on July 3. There was the monogram, KMC, embroidered in gold on the pocket where at least a part of his heart would need to be. All present and correct.

'I'm *alive!* I'm not naked. I'm *me!*'

The matching legs of this garment were defined from the waist, and tight at the ankles, his personal choice of the three brought home by Mother from the land of Hans Christian Andersen.

'A gift of love for my honey-bunny. For when he wishes to gladden the heart of his silly old mère.'

Her coy pronouncement never really declaring that these items were intended for the great out-of-doors.

And what of the Oxford leathers where Earth ended and Knut

began? Slippers, acquired on Mother's pilgrimage to the streets of C.S. Lewis and Lewis Carroll!

This *had* to be a confusing of worlds; mists of the present and mists of the past. Along with the bones.

Knut wishing to discredit the bones. Willing them to vanish. Bones long separated from flesh. Some disarranged. Others as skeletons virtually complete. Four-legged creatures. Others once with wings. Some that could have walked erect.

Knut wishing for his skin to turn to armour.

Down there, over the edge of this ledge, over the face of this cliff or mountain, there remained a mist now stirred by giants, a violence of patterns collapsing and reforming like mandalas in a penetrating silence. These were distances, skies and rainbows as seen only in dreams. Even a fireball, a sun, bursting through an ocean.

What could it be but the crossing of dreams into a place where flesh had become flesh again? A barely visible world of imagined conversations, imagined voices, imagined events, but of real pain turning into a new world with a blinding source of light?

Knut raised his left hand.

'Wearily, I salute the world, whatever world it may be. But what am I to do without my people? Where can they be but somewhere else? I know it from the beat of my heart and the shape of my hand. Just as I know I'm alone and in deep mourning. I show my hand to myself. I clench it. I open it. Yet how can it be there if I'm not real myself?'

Across the back of that tensed hand, veins becoming visible, standing up, he dragged two fingernails and left two wounds turning pale from shock. Almost in the same moment, the same seeing, the same breath, each wound turned purple and bled blood.

CHAPTER
SIXTEEN

THE CRUCIAL
QUESTION

All life is crucial. So, too,
are the dreams.

In time, Knut pressed the back of his hand to his lips, daring to make a Christian sacrament of it.

'Can a spirit bleed?' he asked.

'Does a spirit live among sunrises and bones?

'Who would know a spirit at first meeting? Not that it stops me from knowing what a spirit is not. The knowing is in the genes. The blood sends the message. Take good care of yourself if you're not to become one more skeleton lying among these bones.'

'If I bleed, I cannot be a murdered person. At once I become a *missing* person.

'No one has found me because no one knows where to look. If a passer-by asks the way, do I say, "One step that way to the abyss. Two steps or three any other way and over the edge you go. As for you, so for me."?'

Knut was wriggling back across the flat of his rock, his cliff, his watchtower, or God forbid the top of some disintegrating chimneystack. He was backing away from an edge that could crumble or become a greasy pole or in no solid dimension exist.

'If I don't move again, I can't fall. That's a logic that could please Father.'

Knut was closing his eyes, wishing for no part of him to contact the remains of any dead creature. Drawing up his legs and crossing his arms over them he pronounced, 'Sire, I need to know how I got here!'

The many worlds of humans, of planets, of stars and of gods echoed his question. The Great One God did not reply.

Knut was beginning to rock. Slowly. Fore and aft. Like a supremely anxious child.

It is true: *somewhere* he had seen Hebrew lads at prayer.

BIRD AT A ROADSIDE

Knut calls a spade a spade and
applies for the blessing.

Knut prayed:

'What's dead is dead. Like the bird at the roadside. What's done is done.

'We're not gods, demons or dragons ourselves. We accept that the body dies. All of us, I guess; including the birds. We didn't make the deal, we weren't consulted. Father says it's why people make disasters out of their lives. Though he strives. That's his brand of worship, Sire. It's also mine.

'But we observe that the dead bird flutters his feathers when the wind blows. We have no expectation he'll flutter them at any other time. We observe that his feathers are soon gone with the sun, the wind and the rain. Poor dead bird.

'We observe he's not breaking into nervous sweats as he lies beside the road. We observe he's not asking questions and assume that he's not looking for answers.

'As a mere bird of passage, properly grateful for practically everything, I say that the giving of life and somewhere to live it obligates the giver. Otherwise, we have a moral problem. Father says that truth to oneself is truth in Your presence. Whatever that might mean.

'These are not thoughts of the moment. My parents, birds of a feather with me, would agree. But accepting the idea that if one makes a sentient being, no matter how one goes about it, even if it's fun, there's a sacred obligation to take care of it and to meet its needs. Despite my sentiments when I began my prayer, I'm damned if I can see how that lets You off the hook.

'When I asked my parents for bread and cheese they didn't give me a stone. They didn't set me down among bones. They didn't throw me to the lions. When I asked for love, they overwhelmed me. And they were only human.

'Doesn't God have anything to say?

'At our first serious meeting, I was thirteen. A mild mess, I imagine. I've observed that a mess is par for the course. That sexuality has begun to tear us about and we don't know whether to cheer or to hide.

'At thirteen, I could see two roads. There was a future full of roads, but I saw only two. Mother, I believe, was encouraged that I saw any. The first road was to leave everything to You to fix, taking no account of the mechanics of the Big Bang or of whatever else was on Your plate. Holding You responsible. Requiring You to act. Everything good, bad or frightful being an act of God anyway. Turn it over to You and You'll turn it around to keep the books straight. Squeezing it in between maintaining Galaxy Number One and fine-tuning Galaxy Five Billion and Fifty-eight. By fiddling, retrospectively, with the physics and the clock. No trouble at all when the cry comes from Earth, the beating heart of everyone's favourite galaxy.

'The second road that I saw to the future? Stand square to the wind. Work your own passage. Plot your own course. Steer through the storms of myths, mysteries, marvels and majesties that rage and ache in every bone and chromosome. Make your many mistakes. Draw your few conclusions. In the end get wise or get bushed.

'I told Mother.

'She put a heavy arm on my shoulder. "Honey-bunny," she said, "these ideas in your innocent little head. I can't believe the Lutherans have come to it. Is this my old place of employment? Is this where I pedalled away at the old sewing machine? Is this what they're teaching you now? How exhilarating. It's heresy, my son."

'I said, "It's not an innocent little head, Mother. It's mine. It takes what it needs and remembers what it chooses. It blames no one but itself."

'She said, "Well, pickle me. And all of thirteen! God bless you, my son."

'I'm applying, Sire, for the blessing.

'I believe in Mother. She's shocking people all the time, but I honour her with my heart. And what more can I say of Father that I haven't said before? Along with thanking you for a loving family and loving friends. For cousin Jacqueline. And for Nanette . . . '

Knut was running out of words. He tried again:

'Thank you for Cynthia and of knowing she was with me in a manner of speaking. I'm sorry it was not arranged for her to be born. It is sad that Mother felt she was too old to bear another child.'

Knut, for a short time, was again running out of words. Later, he continued: 'Once Mother said to me that if she'd had this extraordinary child, she wouldn't have called her Cynthia. To which I replied, "Yet you call me Knut and honey-bunny and other things too outrageous to repeat."

'Thank You, Mother, for my thinkings and feelings about practically everything else. Especially for my body. There's nothing I'd seriously challenge except that rotten appendix, though without it I would not have met my little Nightingale. She was great. In case reports got garbled, Sire, she was never really naughty. "No, no, Mr Canute, that's unprofessional." Twice, Sire, she had to say it with the sweetest blush.

'Which brings me to what's been coming since the first hard-drawn breath . . . '

Knut taking his third hard-drawn breath.

'Respectfully, I report an irregularity that leads me to ask whether I'm on the rails or in the rough? From where I sit, bruising on this rock, communing with these bones, it's the worst ride of my life.

'I say last night could not have been served up in judgement, however long the night seemed to be. Judgement for what? For being thirteen and full of it? Or seventeen and full of it? Do You punish me for growing up? You wrote the program. If You don't understand the thrills and the spills, You're not God. In which event, I say, there can be no God.

'I need information, Sire, not stress. I don't want to die of heart failure at seventeen. If I've sprung a trap, why was it set? Why be mean to a kid who'd kept his slate almost squeaky clean? Why, indeed, be mean to one who hadn't?'

Knut allowed a quiet time for clarification or correction. He received none.

'If You hadn't said the magic word long ago and initiated

Creation, none of us would be here, would we? Of a consequence, there'd be nowhere, anywhere. Surely someone must know what happened after I went to bed last night. And why am I sharing this high place with a heap of dead bones?

'I remember what went before; seen in the light at our lovely rosy red end of the spectrum. I ache for her presence, Sire. Is it fair? And I'll not forget my last rites of breaking a couple of eggs and frying them crackly brown at the edges. Putting out dry food for the cats. Taking my shower. Checking the deadlocks. Sire, I know they were locked to everything but the fireman's axe and the key in Father's hand. I remember going up to bed, anxiously. But I hadn't left the wok on high gas. I was raised in an imaginative household where walls were papered with scenarios.

'No more tricks, please, with dates or days. I can't swear to anything by the calendar. I don't know whether last night happened last month or five hundred years ago. I don't know whether my scene is just out of sight or a billion kilometres away. If I had come out of it dead, I would hardly be liking it, but I'd wear it, I suppose.

'But I know that I've come out of it alive and I'm confused.'

THE NATURE OF NATURE

About Fellow Creatures and about time.

Knut had no wish to consider that the prayer of his life might have been ignored. But the past did not encourage him; the silence of the Infinite had never been moved by his prayers on behalf of creatures he assumed to be word dumb. Earthquake prayers, typhoon and tidal wave, volcanic eruption prayers, forest fire and flood prayers, famine and pesticide prayers. Each a cry for creature dignity. Perhaps he had never got it right.

There was a related issue in the use of non-renewable resources on the dinner plate. 'God,' cried Knut, 'You made me a carnivore and set me down among the bones. It's dirty pool.'

At once, flooding his mind, came the memory of the Assembly Hall at Wittenberg College: of the Great Debate of Year Twelve – Pepper Steak and Salad.

Knut's opening statement was delivered on impulse and with passion: 'I'm not a vegetarian!' Marking it with a thrust of the jaw and a pause that provoked hostility down his own side of the hall.

'Though,' he said quietly, 'I wish I were. It's a Matterhorn in my life, a pain, a conflict, a grief.'

Pausing again until the audience understood that he wasn't stuck for words. 'Our Knut,' thought the chaplain, the adjudicator, 'shows uncommon authority.'

'Here and there,' Knut declared, 'among the tins on the supermarket shelf, a few protein foods, products dreamt up by the vegetarians. Not absolutely dead lousy. Imitations of the old hamburger and rack of lamb. Mother's not averse to using one or two. But when she comes up with her peppered steak or chilli chicken or garlic sausages, I have a problem that torments me.'

Knut was again timing his pause with finesse, his voice rising over the cheers from the wrong side of the house.

'Am I or are you to be blamed for race memories of the hunt? Of the fellowship of the campfire? Am I to be blamed for my inheritance and my genes? Does that rule out change? When I start calling the shots . . . When out of respect I'm not bound to compliance in the home of my parents . . .

'Each person here present may count himself or herself the critical witness, prosecutor, judge, jury, court of appeal. When I'm calling the shots, I'll not agree to a death in the family so that I may sit down to a slap-up dinner of animal protein.

'Animals are people.

'Thinking it through knots me in the gut. I share the feeling with others not necessarily on my side of the house. Forget the points score, mates. The issue is greater.'

Knut striking his fourth pause.

'Alternatives. Rejection of Pickwickian tastes that depend upon vegetable additives, anyway. All good things in moderation, except the garlic, the ginger, the chilli, the herbs, the spices.

'When the cow and the goat give me cheese, and the chickens

give me eggs, they don't give short measure. They provide an alternative. My case is mutual dependence. I'm content when our servants and friends, cared for by us, feed us in return, accept our thanks and with dignity walk away. But I suggest we're not half as content as they.

'Keep a respectful distance from edible living creatures if your intentions are not honourable. I think of the steer in the paddock. The deer. The pig in the pen. The hen on free range. The fish in the pond. The duck in the sky.

'Notably, I think of the sacrificial lamb.

'Admire each through your gun sights if you must, but don't make pals of them. Don't sedate your conscience with a few dollars to the wildlife fund if you intend to devour them. They are people with friends, family and sweethearts. Take a close look before your bullet blows out their brains.'

Knut gathered his papers. The chaplain and his fellow speakers, the marginally charmed, the fascinated, the offended – all might as well have been years away.

Knut's official educators instructed him with sensitivity in the continuing ways of a profound and holy Creator. The label *holy* troubled him more than other things. But after a lot of thought and his fourteenth birthday, he questioned comparatively few extras of priestly origin. The clergy had a legitimate vested interest. If they didn't make work for themselves, who would? But Martin Luther was no one's slouch in anyone's century. 'Sir,' Knut said, out of respect.

By parallel standards he was prepared to allow an interval while the Creator framed the response to his prayer. Maybe polish the phrases and check the punctuation and determine whether it should be hieroglyphically expressed. Or broadcast simultaneously in Latin, Hebrew and Ancient Greek. Or in back-street English, burnt with a blowtorch into the tradesman's entrance at the side door to the Universe.

Knut decided the Creator would not paint the reply in the sky with a new extravaganza of rainbows or coloratura smoke trails behind a veteran biplane in the hands of a high-spirited seraph, and would not part the mists either, but might shuffle the cards of time: a curiously alarming idea. He knew that time, for some reason, in some way, was bending or weaving or stretching or striding from place to place. He could *feel* it happening.

Time, he knew, was close to the core of this contract. He didn't care for the contract. He hadn't signed it and hadn't been consulted.

Knut was waiting in the silence as millions beyond numbering had waited in the silence. He went on asking questions set against the abstract components of a Universe that he believed required constant regulation. The science master and the chaplain might have come at it from opposing positions. But not inevitably. Knut knew that when he rode his bicycle he had an eye to the road and a feel for the load. What could the Universe be but the bicycle factor multiplied by the creation factor? If not, the Universe truly was a hall of mirrors.

Further, he often found himself in agreement with the fancy variations on 'eternal truth' as developed by his parents over late-night dinners at the corner of Sebastian and Johann. They were among the more exciting experiences of life. Knut, thrilling and chilling, glancing from parent to parent, adorning the evidence and his love of the people with silent songs that could turn suddenly to fright; a mature appreciation that his father, the architect, past seventy, was at great risk mimicking youth on girders at the fifty-eighth level . . .

Right! *If* the monumental Universe were to be seen as a product of thousands of millions of years, and evolution to be regarded as among Nature's most profound poems, immediate answers to human issues even of life and death were not to be expected in a few dizzying seconds. Humans looking for fairness were obliged to be fair themselves. Humans calling for action were dealing with powers and processes probably alien and were invoking God only knew what.

Knut was entering a phase of acute and pained honesty.

The God addressed by humans in such familiar terms was not made of human clay. Yet humans of intelligence and significant talent went on climbing ladders to paint their idea of his likeness on their ceilings with haloed head and silvered beard. Would such a god, by whatever means, have constructed an unimaginable Universe, or a tinker toy?

At last Knut convinced himself he was obligated to allow an interval between his outgoing call and his hard expectation of reply. He elected to measure it from the ache in his tail that worsened as he swayed on his rock. As a unit of measure, he felt it fair. Whose fault was it he was so spare of flesh and sported a useless tail-bone precisely where he sat?

When he had suffered at his rear more than human nature was intended to bear, he concluded that the answer from on high should have been clear in the heavens or about to impact upon the ear. If not, he dared to conclude it might be time that lesser agencies out there – Planet Watch, Starfax, Express Response – got their act in gear.

Knut was straightening a leg, leaning on an elbow, stretching in several directions and opening his eyes onto a supremely elegant bird.

Too big for a peregrine falcon. Too small for a North American Mustang with Rolls Royce engine. An eagle, Knut thought, or some mythological creature informing me he doesn't approve of my presence on his trophy shelf. This creature hovering in a properly predatory manner. Drifting on breezes. Counter-drifting through spectral shapes of sunlit mist blooming among the leftovers of night.

Thought Knut: Can the hoverings of this bird be language as the cosmics see it? Do they take me for a small boy, hoppedy-skip, with a shoulder bag; a sandwich in it, an apple and a dry pair of pants?

Are they announcing that the young Canute is king of birdland? Or advising that his bones are about to be pecked clean? Or informing him the police chopper's on the way? Or directing him to leap from the brink like a trusting child furiously flapping his laterals prior to flying all the way home to Sebastian and Johann? Which would be First Year stuff for little gods. Intermediate flying training for the kids of middle-ranking gods. But for this kid, a bloody doctorate.

Knut was caught between an unlikely lightness of heart and darkening anxiety.

True, no welcoming word could possibly emerge from the fax machine. Nor any reading of *News and Views at Daybreak* on the TV screen. No morning paper across the breakfast table. No morse code in the earphones. No semaphore flags from ship to shore. No proclamation, limp with paste, drying on the billboard in the square. On the steps of the hall, no town crier. On the king's wall, no writings in fire.

To the great bird, Knut said: 'You could be the answer to my prayer. But the point isn't clear. If it's a property matter, if you hold the deeds to this lip of rock, to this wholly enviable collection of bones, go to the head of the queue. There's no one I'll prefer before you. Just stay high in the sky until I vacate. Venture down here and you'll never know what hit you, mate. I might bag me an eagle for brekky.'

Raw? With my little eye I fail to spy the microwave or the gas barbecue. The primus stove. Even the humble split stick anxious to ignite. With not a match, I swear, to be found alight.

Eagle? Rough-plucked? As poked through the bars by the zoo keeper to *Tyrannosaurus* in Mesozoic times? Around which point of the anatomy do I secure the critical bite? I fear I'd quail even at *Eagle a la Madeleine*. Not that I'd breathe a word of it in her hearing. Mother in the kitchen is the classic female chauvinist screech owl.

Eagle with garlic? With coriander? With birdseye chilli?

What, for example, would I do with fertile eagle eggs on the breakfast plate?

Knut uncomfortably recalled the great debate.

Could I front up with knife, fork and spoon? Down where the beating heart dominates, my opponents would be ranking it with the murder of the little princes in the Tower.

Whereupon, his brittle mood broke.

The break left him fractured, fatigued, tearful, certain that every human he knew was very far off and the line to God was out of order.

...

Hadn't he known, always, that this personal god lived only in the human head? Nature was just too cruel by nature to be anything else.

Nature made Mankind and all other kinds, and when Mankind turned soft, Nature backed off. But when Mankind turned beastly, Nature knew all was well again and withdrew to the ends of time and space to consider new eternal truths, new worlds, new themes, new ideas of space.

Through all the growing pains of growing up, Knut knew. Even listening to the chaplain and the science master, he knew. Even at the dining table so late that the evening looked like night and the night looked like morning. And Knut, though committed to the magic of the mysteries, all the time knowing they were too, too wonderful to be true.

Wailing aloud his own small Hell. His aloneness and his fright. His pain that the prayer of his life was lost, had gone begging, was wandering among the stars looking for an ear so far away it would never hear and wouldn't give a damn if it did.

Life for a raw, two-legged creature of cultivated gentleness, of an oversized brain and the gift of the gab, with unfashionable principles and outmoded moralities, was never more than an after-dinner play with words.

'Mother and Father; if you were trying to be kind, if you were pointing up the magic and the pain, if you were conditioning me to go on being good, whenever and wherever I could, wouldn't it have been better to have beaten me bruised and blue? Then I'd have known and been prepared.'

This was the moment of realising that he was in the presence of an exquisite cat; a leopard misted in the morning; as a fish of prey might appear among stray beams of light striking through masses of weed in a clouded lake.

Knut was shocked and shaking, at the extreme edge of disbelief; a breath short of hysteria; at a perilous frontier beyond which nothing more could be borne. But out of which, suddenly, mercifully, he found himself able to laugh at the absurdity of the world and at the absurdity of trying to make order out of chaos with mere words. At which the leopard dissolved like the fish of prey sliding from the light back into the darkest depths of weed.

For a time, Knut became calm and reflective and gave consideration to the nature of laughter.

CRITICAL POPULATION
EXPLOSION DAY

*Knut contemplates the nature of
the Universe he has entered and
why he is the one who's been
displaced.*

All Hell breaking loose all around.

Knut was on the swings again.

'I've seen rainbows,' he said. 'I've seen the sun come up. I've seen lakes and mists and seas. I plead with High Heaven; it ignores me. I need to know what has happened to me! How *can* I be dead? I tear at myself and bleed.

'One thing this condition of mine cannot be. It cannot be a dream. I'm in deep space somewhere, but haven't I always been? Could I not be the sole male inhabitant of a new world? God only knows how far away from me my Nanette must be. I'll be looking for her. She'll be looking for me.

'Or have I been nobbled by greasy human reptiles lurking in my own sacred house at the corner of Sebastian and Johann? And from there conveyed to this place. Which means they passed the deadlocks and the alarms. No way in through the roof or down the chimney or up the laundry chute or by dematerialisation.

'The stickers on windows and doors declare:

It's the fool
who breaks in here
where angels fear
and devils tread.

'All these years and never a hero. But someone was there to nobble me. Which suggests an inside job.

'Okay. Let's face it. What reason would Father have? And would Mother do away with her honey-bunny because my girlfriend is not to her liking?

'Who else could get through? Who else could find the switch in twenty seconds before the alarm triggers and we have bedlam running wild?

'Hell, I say . . . Hell.'

When Knut dared to be himself again, he thought:

I was walking my darling home. Then walking myself home. Embracing the pavement. Scrambling the eggs. Taking the shower. Climbing the stairs. Removing the incrimination with care and imagination . . . But I had dragons in wait somewhere. I'm well briefed on dragons. I'm the son of an authority.

But do I raise Cain? Do I blacken eyes or break heads? Do I draw my rapier and drive them from the house? Bloody no. I go like the sacrificial lamb.

Father, do make the effort to keep the peace with the police. Curly Canute, ancestor or not, wasn't worth it all those years ago. If he had robbed you as he robbed the lady and groped you in the same breath, you'd have broken his bloody neck.

110

Your house was booby-trapped to knock 'em witless, but you cry that Curly holding up the coach was the victim of the State. Be consistent. Spare a thought for your son, groped with needle or gun when all I was doing was dreaming of my girl? And you, sir, and your lady were supping at Susannah's celebrating my conception.

If all this is so, how did they get me onto this ledge?

Am I in Kakadu or the Kimberley? Am I in Arabia?

How do I explain the autumnal mists? Did they drop me from a chopper? Shoot me from a howitzer?

Father, poke a finger in your ear and wiggle out the wax. Tell me, was it ever so warm in our kind of country at this time of year? I submit, six thousand k's, at least, or a few light years must lie between thee and me and the edge of my door at the top of the stairs.

I ask you people, you dragons, you demons, you bloody Gnomes, why waste money on a kid like me? Whose problem at MI5 am I likely to solve?

Whose ziggurat did I build?

In exchange for freedom, whose marble forecourt can I conceive or construct?

Father, why didn't they make the hostage of you? How could they mistake a kid for an old bloke of seventy-two?

Knut was at last beginning to realise that the fogs coming and going in his head had something to do with the sun. It appeared to be standing at around forty degrees high. So, were time and space not as they had been? Might his sun as he saw it now truly be a star he didn't know? Might he, along with all thinking creatures, have been cut off in an instant from all others and switched via a cosmic malfunction, a mischievous play, or a new creation myth, to another mode?

Were these the bones of recognisable creatures? Was the leopard a phantom, the eagle the same? Was the source of light and heat the sun that he had known? Was the mist truly a mist? Was the atmosphere air?

Had every creature able to believe in an abstraction of any kind been torn from one world and set down in another, allowed neither the time nor the means to report it or record it?

On one such new world, Father? On another, removed by multiples of light years, Mother? What had they done to deserve severance from each other?

Who deserved the earthquake or the fire storm? Who deserved to be born grossly disadvantaged?

How many persons like Father and Mother and Aunts Sophie and Ingrid, and cousins Jacqueline and Claus, and Nanette and Knut could the gods rip apart and instantly provide with habitable planets for solitary confinement?

How many human-like creatures could there be for the gods to disperse in such an arbitrary moment? Were the projections brought up to date every century or so? Billions of planets coming on line at the declaration of each Critical Population Explosion Day? Was each new world commissioned by the ceremonial delivery of the *Word*? Initiated by the sigh around the conference table? Bringing into service the galaxy currently held in readiness to absorb the offspring of the ever-busy human-like creatures to be found throughout the Universe – behind every curtain and door, every haystack and cow bale, every kind of cabbage and copse of trees, every tussock of reed and bulrush, boulder and pot-hole, rosebush and opened broadsheet of evening news and inaccessible holy places?

Well, given but one condition or all, the gods couldn't escape a twinge of responsibility.

They could've arranged for propagation by other means. Pot culture, thought Knut. A nice little cutting. A finger or toe. In a plastic pot in a wrought-iron box to catch the morning sun outside the bedroom window. The definitive form of population control.

In terms of eternity, might the explosive effect of human reproduction be the cause of galactic proliferation? A tempting idea for the brain bank to kick around.

Countless thousands of millions of new worlds made available, regularly, at ever-distancing fringes of the Universe, not specifically to drive astronomers, physicists and theologians insane, but to accommodate the magnitude of displaced persons so recklessly generated, willy-nilly, hey-nonny-nonny, hip-hip-hooray, let's have another glut of birthdays . . .

Each new planet would be a nunnery, a monastery, a hermitage, an eagle's eyrie, a leopard's lair, a royal throne for one unaccompanied human.

'Father of gods,' Knut said, 'is this what You started with that Big Bang?'

KNUT AS MONARCH
OF THE WORLD

*Knut is reminded that the
making of realities is a
worthy life.*

HAIL, KING CANUTE, monarch of this brand new world for
one celestial day! Be aware that the game continues to be
time – the use of it and the thrust of it. So, long life to you.
Live for ever. Be one of us. Welcome to the club.

If the outcome proves to be for the better, your world shall
endure and all unborn generations will bless your realm by
continuing to remain unborn.

God save the king!

May all the gold and treasures of the soil, all the tuna of
the sea, multiply in glory and riches for thee.

But, if the outcome proves to be for the worse . . . ! In the
unlikely and unseemly event of your union with some en-
thusiastic female consort! Be warned! Though we take comfort that not even the Great God knows or shows where such
a creature may be!

Be warned! She shall terminate your immortality forthwith
and the last generation of your blood line, as it goes down in
deprivation thousands of generations hence, scarcely with

space to occupy, or room to scratch, or air to breathe, or food for the table, shall prefix your names with curses and add the suffix:

ADAM AND EVE, MAKERS OF THE ADAM BOMB.

Well, thought Knut, are we to consider this barren place, hemmed about by its mysteries and its mists, to be the garden of Eden? And am I to be Adam all dressed up in a fine pair of slippers and royal blue pyjamas?

I ask, pointedly, what of Eve?

If love and logic are eternal, if this disturbing thought holds its germ of truth, two persons displaced and dispersed may well have been exiled to this kingdom, each prepared to seek the other, each accepting that life and love must end or cannot exist at all. Knut and his Eve, each agreeing to the mortal state. Why not? Father calls it the divine equation. The self-righteous declare it to be original sin.

So Knut went on peering into the depths of his new horizons, where the mists were assuming a splendid motion for the entertainment of himself the king. Mists were elevating in billows and clouds and streamers and threads, as if bound for that most distant and ultimate vacuum where the gods guarded their silences. Where the galaxies were oiled on their axes, and 'decibel', since the Big Bang, had become an obscene word.

The vista Knut could see opening up appeared to be a lake of unfractured calm. A great lake with only one visible shore, Knut's own mountain. In its turn, it was an odd sort of mountain isolated in an odd kind of lake. A lake as big as a country might dare to be in an overcrowded world. Which meant that

Knut's barely habitable ledge on his mountainside might need to be regarded as prime real estate.

'Seventeen years aged in the wood,' Knut said of himself, 'bottled in maternal winter weights with KMC on the label. Master of his personal planet? Indeed. Canute the First rules the waves, monarch of all that he surveys. Not a commoner in sight unless I propagate my own. Well, kings have made a life's work of it. What say you, King Louis, King Henry, King Solomon?

'And thee, King Canute, thou modest Dane, a thousand years removed if my calendar hasn't changed. On English sand, your robes like mine supplied by Copenhagen, bidding the tide to turn around to prove that it wouldn't. No man's fool, our modest Dane. No man's fool, either, shall I be.

'If Knut Canute rules these waters that I see, whose waters were they before me?

'I also wonder about a moon. I shall have one. By decree, if necessary. My loyal subjects in the paddocks shall not be billing and cooing, unable to see the beauty of the other. Nor shall I whilst begetting them in the first instance.

'Is it not logical to assume I would be alone on my planet without an Eve? Why create a monarch to entertain a bird? Absurd. Why a king for a disappearing cat? Why a Khan for a heap of bones? There must be a tower and a princess. Or a queen in search of her consort. Mother and Father made clear that perfection lies between these extremes. It was a truth they demonstrated, they say, when their love made me, adding, "The cosmos is a divine equation initiated by woman and man".'

So Knut found himself able to stand back from himself, far enough away to smile a little from relief. There to hear from within himself a small voice: 'I am here because I have to be and because I am.'

We're linked, Nanette and I. She is the other half of me as I am the other half of her. If there's nothing of her, there can be nothing of me, except for an irrational minute here and there and an occasional word. If she proves not to be my Eve, what shall I do? The gods must surely know I'll die if I cannot breathe the air that comes through her to me. Why is it that among the millions there is only one I wish to see? What can either of us be but shadows exiled to the ends of the Universe? I swear and decree, that each shadow shall seek the other.

Richard Canute was fifty-seven before he found his Madeleine.

Was Mother his second? Or his four hundred and fifty-second? Was he her fifth or fifty-fifth?

Mother says first sweethearts are in love with dreams. Her ways are not my ways. She's not my Holy Writ. She might be half of her own divine equation, but she is not the prophet of mine.

There must be a better place than this. Some safer place. Or is this all that gods and men have left for me?

Am I to build a raft and make its paddle and stitch its sail without timber, tools, canvas or thread? Do I wait for Jonah's whale? Do I hope for Noah cruising past?

I have a cliff for my safe place. No known way down; no known way up; no known way back to where I came from. It's my desert island, as impossible to reach as it is to abandon. But does this mean I cannot try? Who was it that made the door at the top of the stairs admired by Father? Not bloody Bill.

'An interesting door,' Father said. 'Most pleasing. Are you dead set on statistics, son? The making of realities is a worthy life. If I have not been misled, civilisation was carved out of dead wood.'

There came a time when Knut thought: How broad might my kingdom be? How long? How many square Edens to comb before I find Eve? Or Eve finds me?

If I climb the mountain, if I dare, what do I come upon? Rocks that fall? Slopes that crumble?

If I go down, is it to crocodiles and tropical fevers?

If I stay where I am, do I make a meal for a leopard and become another heap of bones?

If I do nothing, if I sit and meditate, to what am I exposed? Are gun sights trained on me?

The splendour of this response to prayer is a calamity. I asked for answers. I am given a guessing game.

A year ago I hadn't focussed on Nanette. But she was there. Down the street and up the lane and around the corner, as invisible as next year.

Who was set on that Old Time Night in that old time church hall for the kids of her school and mine? No one but the old timers. Spider webs in the rafters. Quartered sandwiches in the kitchen. Cordial. Tap water. Tea. And Horace Hopper's Twentieth Century Dance Band dating from 1943.

If I hadn't caught sight of her then, would any of this have happened? If our meeting had never happened, would 1.17 a.m. have hit me just the same? Say it had hit me when I was twelve. Twelve like Manfred two doors down. Could anyone do to Manfred what's been done to me? Thank God I wasn't twelve. Thank God I wasn't seventy-two.

Events of the kind, they tell me, are chiselled in the rocks and written in the scrolls. In the myths and legends and history books. Upon events such as these, I've heard them say, we've made our way through the ages.

Knut recalled dinner table wisdom from the corner of Sebastian and Johann: 'Do not delude yourself, young Canute. What may outrage the humans, may not even be of minor concern to gods. If gods there be. If there are no Powers to hold the Universe together, no God or gods, there is no one, there is nothing anywhere, that'll give a damn about you or me.'

Same dinner table scene, same speaker at much the same time: 'God isn't likely to be alone out there any more than we are here. But never come to hope that the gods are as we are.'

And so Knut was struggling across a threshold of understanding; a monstrous and terrifying alternative; that he of all Humankind might be the only one thus confined and condemned to the state of being Adam without Eve.

CHAPTER
TWENTY-ONE

A GAME PLAYED BY
THE MASTERS

*Knut thinks of theories concerning
how he got to where he is:
the game seems to be time itself.*

Knut was warned suddenly, instinctively, not knowing of what. He was looking up and catching an image of the great bird plunging from above like a winged missile, passing through his vision with dark belly and swept wingspan, all too close through several fractures of a second.

At what point was it that the wingspan fanned and shot the great bird back to a height beyond human seeing? Or was that a mere imagining? Had it, like an arrow, vanished from his vision into the unmarked lake or sea as large as a country might be, that monumental vastness of marsh or mud or mist?

What could Knut recall with conviction other than the rush of wind? In moments he was holding hard to a crude idea that God was stating He had faith in Knut to solve his own problems. 'Go down,' God appeared to say, 'if you wish. Or, alternatively, go up.'

'You're not talking to Father,' Knut cried, 'I'm not seventy-two. How would You know what it's like to be seventeen? Or seventy-two either?'

...

Later, Knut asked, 'Would going down be a plausible way of starting a new world? What of losing my grip and plunging into the pit? Stupid bloody idea. Bouncing from rock to rock till I hit bottom.'

I can't seriously reckon I've been carried off by aliens. How many light years is it from *any* star with a planetary system to the corner of Sebastian and Johann?

Can you hear them at every crossroad and Cloud of Magellan?

Which way to Earth?

'Earth? What would that be, for pity's sake?'

Is there anything I remember that could've been a journey through time or across distances that no one understands except the gods and the Einsteins?

I might remember express trains through tunnels. And a sacrificial smell that could have been the burning of me. But my Abraham wasn't home from *The Turn of the Screw*. That dreadful old man was quaffing red at Susannah's or hailing a cab because neither he nor his lady could remember where they'd parked the tank.

Billingsgate! Now why would aliens, on dry land after a million years in transit, be talking stupid in English? More likely they'd be dancing and cavorting in the streets. Carrying on like fishwives at the Canute front gate? Hardly, my friends. Hardly.

Was it a short circuit? A cosmic overlap? Or by chance? Disconnected incidents, years and lives apart, coming together for a second or two a great distance from their points of origin? Why not? Everything's big enough.

Alternatively, does the Universe go out of phase while my life grinds through a change of gear? Or did the tide really run back for King Canute and no one's ever been game to say it?

Was the water, thundering on my windowpane, in reality a coolant for combustion chambers? Might it have had nothing to do with Father's fire hydrant or hyped-up V8s with P plates crashing through the crossroads? It could've been a lift-off. A bit rough and ready. But what manner of mess would it have left at the corner of Sebastian and Johann? A bloody great black hole?

If you set out to cross the light years to kidnap a dumb kid, you need a few refinements like immortality and anti-gravity propulsion. Together with a prediction of births, deaths and marriages on planet Earth to cover the several biological ages you're in transit.

I did give thought to an aircraft booby-trapped for take-off. Even considered a firing squad. But if ratbags like that were in power, would they bother to execute a kid? They'd just dig a hole and chuck him in.

And what of the warlords and bandit kings? Would they do this to Father, through me, to secure his services?

'Why do I fascinate these creeps?' Father says. 'Do I smell like a sullage pit? I should have botched my beautiful ziggurat and designed garden gnomes with red noses. Should've answered the call to the priesthood that came ringing through the night: *Richard! Hearest thou me?* But I turned the other way and fell out of bed and branded my brow on a brandy glass. I wasn't born with this cleft between the eyes.'

And where, considered Knut, do I fit my spooky lady? Be calm. Be still, she said. Between the abyss and me, I've been considering Grandmother Mannerheim and hearing her cry of long ago as she dropped from the mountain. Knut, Knut, Knut! But who could go for an idea like that?

Aloud, Knut said: 'Sire, I'm still waiting on an answer to my prayer. Are You dead set on leaving me lumbered with abysses and eagles and bones and the ghosts of leopards and of God knows what else?

'How did they bring me here?

'How many more times must I ask?

'And where's my lovely mum?

'I want my half-coddled curried egg.

'I'm hungry. I'm frightened. I'm all on my own.'

Might there have been a reply from the core of the Universe, as removed to its farthermost skin? 'Join the club, dear boy. It's lonely here, too.'

IN THE DOORWAY, THE PALE PAWN

Knut realises he is the one who holds the key to the door of the world.

Was the edge of Knut's cliff an issue, a lure, a trap? Or there because it had to be somewhere? This shelf on the cliff face, this leftover of a landslip or a machine-driven cut, this decomposing brim with an edge that was so close. Does a crumbling world serve notice that it wishes to move again?

Above the irregular line of this brink were the distances of Knut's featureless lake and misted sky. Below the line lay the abyss, lay everything he couldn't see and in which there might be greater security. Might it be safer to go down with the slip than to bring it thundering upon his head? Or was he ignoring a principle already debated, already resolved, that going down to start any kind of world was not the way for him. Yet he went, worming on chest, hips and knees, thrusting with his feet, extending his fingertips to their uttermost reach. Feeling the way. Every conscious part of him fearing that the earth might move. Which of course it did.

He sickened; his will died within him. He waited without feeling until he was icy cold and breathing so lightly he felt faint.

124

Little by little he then edged back with meticulous care until he was hard against the wall with nowhere to go. A jutting lip now concealed what lay above, just as that other lip had concealed everything below.

Unknown depths and unknown heights, opposed. Neither to be negotiated by him. No ropes. No pitons. No snap-links. No crampons. No stirrups. No fellow climbers. No helping hand or steadying word. Five hundred metres to the top at least. Could have been five thousand. An eagle's way up and a spider's way down. The curse of these Mannerheims and their Matterhorns.

Knut said within himself: What am I but a pawn in a game played by masters. A knee into the edge of the table scatters their kings and queens and knights and bishops. Why is it that everyone fails to observe the pale pawn in the doorway that could have won the game?

Mother dear, if God can't come because He's too busy, what's wrong with *you*? When did I ask you last to come to my aid? Did I ever? Or did I never?

Once upon a time at a midnight table at the corner of Sebastian and Johann, this same Madeleine said: 'Only God may tell how many marvels and miracles have run aground since the first few humans placed hand to hand and petitioned the sun, the moon, the stars and the Matterhorn. Marvels and miracles that never happened, my son, because individuals even as bold as your father were too timid. Marvels and miracles as numerous as all the humans since humans began. Among us there isn't one of healthy mind, even you, even me, who cannot move the stars.'

It's to be hoped someone took it farther, that someone said to Knut, then or later, that he could confront God if he wished.

That God would not strike him down. That God's way had never been like that. He was not a God of vengeance but a God of compliance. He had set Mankind free. He meant it and was stuck with it.

Knut, by demonstrating his strength, could be master of his fate instead of its slave. He could be the Adam of his Eden or its serpent, its dragon or its fool, as he chose. But only by recognising that he possessed the same freedom to flex muscle as gods on the roar like Ra and Zeus and Shiva and Thor. Gods created by Mankind. What more?

Yet, for all of that, Knut must go the way he's supposed to go of his own free will, or he'll end up like Father with a cleft in his brow, unless his brow already bears that scar.

If Knut uses his freedom not to exercise his power, he obscures his horizons and buries, as if he were a dead thing, the young man who could have come to flower. And so loses his chance to be Adam, to be king, to aspire to be a Luther. Even endangers his choice not to be a Hitler.

ALONE ON THE THRONE

Knut says NO to the axe, but
YES to the guillotine.

Around high noon of one day or another, Knut noted uneasily that he was drifting in and out of himself, as if observing himself from a distance. This could have been occurring for some time; his brain functioning without the sharper edges, drifting into confusion. Hunger was of no importance, but thirst could have become a problem and his head was full of leftovers from other days and other years.

Of course, he told himself, it must be the sun up there. But why so high in the sky? It's not appropriate to the season. It seems but a day or two since we waxed our skis, readying for Year Twelve's traditional big weekend. Hi ho. Of which am I not my mother's souvenir of eighteen years ago? Eighteen or eight hundred? Eight thousand or a million or two? Who cares?

Well, if it's not the sun that dazzles me, am I under the anaesthetic, under the knife again, under the light? Which raises further questions, indignantly. Why have I come round in the middle of it? I am astonished that my little Nightingale has not leapt to comfort me?

You over there with the piercing black eyes and the white side whiskers and the big curly tail, what are you pussy-footing

127

around for? There's nothing in this contract requiring me to see the show. Father's paying you people a great deal of money to keep this operating theatre entirely concealed from my view. While at home across the table at the corner of Sebastian and Johann, they'll be discussing my genes, no doubt, as if they were gold plated. They have a vested interest in self-deception, especially when they send me in for repairs.

Well, if they call them genes, I call them fit for flushing out with the sump oil. Kindly do so before you insert the new gasket and bolt me together again. Yet the longer I flinch under this light, the more I believe it comes up in the morning and sets again at night . . .

I'm round the twist . . . Delirious . . .

God. Pull yourself together, mate.

Knut raised himself on an elbow.

Full sun. Sky high. Gorgeous beach weather but not a seashell in sight. And no girls. Not even a retired school principal with sunglasses walking his beagle. Strange.

A hazed world all around with glazed levels of blued grey and white, suggesting the idle metaphor of a former insect dislodged from pages tightly closed long ago. Hot as Hell back there between the pages, but a bloody sight worse out here.

I *must* do something about me. Drastic action, if the House of Canute is not to be declared kaput. Present indications are that extinction is the official line. I observe no rush from any quarter to serve the king.

'It is clear,' Knut said within the stresses of his brain, 'that I rule alone on my throne, king only of me. In view, there is no approaching Crusade. No Charge of the Light Brigade. No

Relief of Mafeking. No little Mustang taking off between the palms. The person of Knut Mannerheim Canute is an abandoned rag hanging by a peg while everyone else trips off to happyland. But if you have a valuable specimen like me, don't you switch on the life-support system and chuck it a can of beans and a bottle of fizz? Do you abandon it to the crows? You'll get nothing for a bag of bones. You'll do better with a bag of rags. Wouldn't it have been neater and sweeter if you people, whoever you are, had hit me on the head and chucked me in the lime pit as you used to do and quietly walked away?

'Oh dear. Oh dear. I'm scared.

'I say again, I'm not about to pick a path down this little hill. Abysses are for poets and politicians, not for kids. I'm goin' up without pitons or crampons and sticking like a mussel to everything I touch. I've got to get out of here. Climbing this Matterhorn like I never climbed trees with cousin Claus. Claus and me, sitting up there, swinging our legs, swaying on our little bit of wind; not a thought to how hard the world down there might be if a branch cracked and we dropped.

'Would Claus know me any more? Would my darling, if our paths crossed? If I said, "Nanette, my sweet; it's me, it's me," would that odd, that dear, dear old-fashioned girl hurry away?

'There was a prayer, I believe, once spoken by me. It seems to have lost its way. Too far to go, I suppose. Or God was too busy swinging new deals and holding press conferences and launching new galaxies and kissing babies and cooking up new models of the human idea. So who do we blame when I fall? Who foots the bill? Who feels the hurt? The buck, young Canute, stops right here.'

...

Later. Days later or years later, who knows? It was a time of crisis with Knut slamming into his prison wall in sudden rage, striking at it with hands and heels, berating himself. Beat your brains out on it, mate. Going up or down it'll be the same. As usual, your life will be hanging out like a bit of rag. Take the flying leap over the edge. Cut the losses. Clean the slate. Leave the outcome to the sweet drop.

An alternative viewpoint simultaneously originated with Father, like a voice issuing from the muscles of the thighs, a familiar shape solidifying in the shadows of Knut's brain and declaring: 'What have I begat? Where's the native wit? Where's the young god? Impregnated in the grain at the edge of that door? Go for the new perspective: pursue the architectural solution of the ziggurat long ago prepared. Note that imminent head-on collisions come to nothing at the roundabout.'

'They do at my roundabout,' Knut said. 'You're not there.'

Later yet, at a time of less stress, perhaps in the cool of an evening, Knut quietly worked a short distance along the cliff face out of which his shelf had been formed. He picked his path through, over, or behind the bones of eagles, sparrows and mice. Perhaps of deer, zebra and rhinoceros. Or of geese and Babylonians, avoiding contact with all and each as if every one had perished of the Black Death.

He moved, in all, about thirty metres. There meeting a mischief of nature; a visible break in the body of the mountain as if once split by explosives and poised ever since to roar into the abyss. Driving him to retreat to his starting point; then to go beyond it until he was stopped by another split in the face of the mountain.

An irritable image of Father briefly appeared like the leopard, only to fade in the same manner: 'Architecturally,' the image said, 'I don't intend to be proved wrong by you or any mindless mass of matter.'

Knut responded by giving the mountain the extra kick it deserved. But at once regretting it, for it was clear that the surface was so unstable that it left him caked with dust from head to foot.

Was it not a mountain at all? Was it just a heap of chalk?

An entertaining or terrifying thought?

Was the world about to break up and blow away? Or was it the dust of his own body? Were his own precious dusts unto dust returning?

Knut converting this idea into a cry. 'What's it got to do with me, anyway? What shocking awful thing did I ever do? I honoured my father and mother!'

So bone weary, so brain weary, so low.

Coming together again. Wishing to view his mountain; its contours and features. To see what it was and what it was not. He was uncertain how to approach the problem; flight not being possible, he believed, whilst still dragging a body around.

Knut was then making an effort to project himself on to the summit of his mountain, to see it, stretching for its Garden of Eden, for its logic and its reason. Imagining its drinking fountains, fire hydrants and crossroads. Its cab ranks, railway stations and airports. But public facilities up there, along with everywhere else, would be available only to persons with cash in hand. As ever, the Universe to one against.

As for each bone in his immediate view, he saw it as a memory, discarded and left to bleach in wind, rain and sun.

There to reside among the last runners of every last race of all other days, years and centuries. All these tiny souls in endless line astern, thrown one by one to the Great Lion of the Universe.

Knut bogging down in the thought. Of all the games of chance, this was the most ancient; the lone spirit against creation. This place, this was the end of the fall. This was the ledge at the end of the world. Here were the creatures who had tried to climb the mountain of life before.

Knut crying aloud: 'But I'm only seventeen!'

Which, mercifully, redirected his imaginings to the day, to the evening of his turning seventeen. Mother was there. As were the cats. Cousin Claus was there and cousin Jacqueline. Aunts Sophie and Ingrid. Father was in Honolulu on a building site, striding back and forth, laying down the law on level forty-four – and Nanette was at home. Not invited. Brooding in her room with her tears on the day Knut turned seventeen.

'Mother had no right to disapprove of her; but she sure had the nerve! The things that lady did to me. I never would have stood for it if I had not honoured her.'

Was Knut not the one who swung the debates and scored the runs and kicked the goals when the outcome was looking grim? When they won, was he not the hero of the fight, the one they called the buckle of the belt? But where were the same guys at party time? Why couldn't Knut name one or two who would really like to come and wouldn't cause problems because they had?

A last pale presence of the father image laid a brief hand upon him: 'A warning, young man, of the failure of information to inform. The majority can be right, but not when it's scared. Go for the architectural solution.'

With that, Knut, too, took his leave, mentally, from the scene and slept.

The world to which he returned, not knowing when, was no longer blued or greyed. It was like a world at the rosy red end of the spectrum. A boy-and-girl coloured world, Knut's own hands having acquired a related hue. His arms to the elbows, his Copenhagen pyjamas, his Oxford leathers, even the soles of his feet for all he knew.

Might this mountain have been of rust rather than of chalk? Rust like the dust of the hurts and pains of human things? Or was it coloured by a drop of blood lodged between his eyes and the brain?

Could, at this moment, the sun be setting in a blaze of flame? Oh, the perils of the religious education.

And what am I but bloody seventeen?

If I do in fact manage a hundred moves up there on the face of this mountain, even five hundred before my luck runs out, will fate leave me clinging by the fingertips? Dusk falling? Night falling? With Knut falling, too?

Oh, these Mannerheims and their Matterhorns. They didn't leave us their money, which Mother says would've been handy. They left us their bad luck and the maintenance of their tombs.

'I,' said Knut, 'prefer to go out like the king who says NO to the axe but YES to the guillotine.

'The king, Mother says, is more, as well as less, than human. Beware, she says, of kings and queens who rule by right of birth. Honour them. Be aware of what they are. Each is the continuity of a thousand years. Each is your birthright as well as theirs.'

Knut's thinkings were the splashings of storms.

'The night I disappeared, with the clock at 1.17, life picked me up and put me down as if I were a book not to be read with a tired brain. I could never have made a fight of it. It's stupid to think that I could have done. It was a crisis night that cost me even my love Nanette.'

Knut with feelers, with feathers, with animated skin, thudding his fists into his mountainside again, as if striking it with his body on the way down. Interesting idea. But Father had said that going down was not the architectural solution.

What day is it back in that other Universe where life used to be? If Tuesday, its last period is Latin. If Wednesday, it's *The Canterbury Tales*. If Thursday, it's Miss Rosenbaum and Hebrew Principles of Language and Feeling.

'I say Thursday!'

Elapsed time since Tuesday 1.17 a.m. is seriously amounting to *what*? Have I spent several days or a great number in some new Universe? Or has it been but one demented swing of the pendulum through a chaotic shuffling of the brain?

'Might I be strapped to my bed? Restrained?

'Does some person sit on my chest to hold me down, for I cannot get my breath? Why must I have to fight for it? Why must I seem to fall? Because I am!

'I mean, I bloody am!

'Finally, finally, I fall and have no idea how it occurred. What did I bloody do that went wrong?'

LAMENT

*If you didn't mean me to
complain, why fill me with
brain?*

Knut began to address God most urgently. Not aloud, for each word flew on wings of lightning, and passed by, and vanished in seconds.

Well, I've always known I was going to fall. Have I not? But did it have to come so soon?

It's a landslide, I guess, and I'm the cause of it and in the middle of it. It was in the program. Who wrote the program?

Not I.

I've always known I wasn't made to stand unless I went on shouting the command. From age fifteen months, shouting it continually. The moment I forgot to be in charge the fall began.

An addendum, Sire, to that foolish little prayer of mine that must have stayed right here among the bones. I pray I'm falling out of bed at the corner of Sebastian and Johann. I don't care what day or year. I don't care if I wake up five years old or fifty.

Are You hearing anything from me away down here? I have to wonder. Mountain and sky and You have shown marked disinterest in me.

I've climbed mountains, Sire, often. Respectfully, as one of a team. As you would know. Giving respect where it was due. But now I'm on my own and making new rules. If You hear scream-ing from down here, I won't be screaming at the mountain. The mountain had no say in it. I'll be screaming at You.

I gather You've been around since the first idea. It's got me beat how You put up with it, but who better to propose the new idea of a few living creatures to cultivate the garden for You to walk among in the quiet of the evening. Each little creature endowed to generate a few more to keep the plot growing as the elders withered and returned to the soil. As for You, You'll still be ticking along when everything else is gone.

I was always perishable, born that way, but if You didn't mean me to complain, why fill me with brain? To cushion the fall? Or to go on parroting to the last gasp, Glory to the great God on high? Like I'd be burning in Hell if I didn't?

That theme was tuning me out before I got to sixteen. I have, Sire, an enormous opinion of You and soon knew that mindless magnification added only to Your embarrassment. But You were stuck with it. Were you not? Because You had given humans the right to think as they pleased. And the people were stuck with it because the priests had been working at it, night and day and centuries between. Threatening God alone knew what if we didn't tow the line. And the priests were as free to threaten as were we.

When I worship, wouldn't You rather I held my head high, proud to have been made by You by one magic or another? Or would You rather I grovelled and called myself wretched and renegade and rotten because a few characters with a vested interest in everlasting punishment were telling me You'd fry me if I didn't? Were telling me I was damned because I'd been *bad* dozens of times, though thousands of times I had striven to be good.

What have You given me that I can count upon when I hit the rock bottom of this fall any millisecond from now?

I have not had time to scream.

I can't even be sure I'll see You then, from a long way off. I've been told it's not on. I don't even know if I just cease to be. I don't even know if being born is not the beginning but the end.

I wait for an explanation, Sire, but You'll need to be quick. Why should the One Great God ignore what's been done to me? Am I not one of Your children? Though there was a time when six million Jews and twenty million Russians and indigenous peoples beyond number world-wide were asking the same question.

A REASON FOR
THE FALL

*Knut debates about his
preferred companion, the
hound.*

Knut's voice, silent of late, returned with blunt authority: 'By God. I'm not falling any more.'

Knut was checking back to sources through the forests of his mind.

'I don't remember at the end of the fall coming to the stop, but no one's going to tell me I didn't make the drop!'

Knut deliberately counting two hands, two feet and a functioning head attached to a middle still stuck to its ends. Which meant he was not dead and had not sprouted wings as of angels or blue wrens – confirmed by the creeping of a hand into his back; exploring for flight muscles and feathers, but lacking the resolution to force his eyelids apart.

A turn was in the air. All around it went on turning, like the morning and the evening of the sixth day when God considered good all things that had been made.

No, thought Knut. Let's keep it simple.

Thereupon, a creature (bird, beast or myth) added a sound to the scene that left Knut with palpitations, causing him to wonder if he had heard it from somewhere underground.

I thought, thought Knut, that the big cats roared and in between slept a lot. I thought they didn't act the fool, but spent hours in shady places stripping flesh from bones. I should've spent more study time at the zoo. I'd feel less threatened if people like the leopard purred like the Russian Blue. But what is it that makes the sound of the hound? Surely nothing that is not very closely attuned.

The hound, thought Knut, eats bones and all. Much to be preferred. Would he have left this ridge of bones to disturb and unnerve me? No. No. Never. As he rushes out to play what does he leave behind but a few harmless heaps of poo. A mere dozen or two. Much less disturbing than bones.

Thus innumerable hounds come to mind. Hounds of Heaven and of Earth, and of late I regret to relate, some of the hounds of Hell.

Exhilarating hounds. Boring hounds. Brutish hounds. Over-the-fence hounds. Next-door hounds. Those of scent and of sight. Even those with cosmic opinions. Each giving me the eye as he passed by, striving to slip his lead. How come that hounds and I, so enchanted by one another, have been thwarted at every attempt to establish a liaison?

I fear we need look no farther than this mother of mine.

I'd turned ten . . .

Rushing home, woof woof, the length of Sebastian Street, that splendid red setter and I. Though he was grey and it's true I'd wondered why.

On a later day, the dauntless dane. Well, dane of a kind. There'd been an affair, I understand, with a dashing German wirehaired pointer.

On a later day still, of hope and goodwill, there was I like a sled downhill, towed through the gate by the Alaskan Malamute whose mother had adventured with a whale.

Later yet, deferentially, introducing the pyrenean, the prince incognito, due to the numerous indiscretions of his immediate relations. Then eye to eye and nose to nose with the awesome Irish wolfhound whose devoted parents had been faithful to the end. NO. Mother screeching from all compass points simultaneously, completing the maternal siege.

'Two Russian Blues wherever we put our feet! Whose cats are they?'

'Mother, cats have nothing to do with my handsome newfoundland, one of whose recent ancestors, I admit, might have dallied with a poodle.'

'You heard the question. Whose cats?'

'Everybody's cats, Mother. As everybody at this address has always known.'

'How generous of you,' Mother continued. 'How kind. But *which* everybody among us made the promises and did the nagging? *Who* negotiated the deals? Were you not of a responsible age? With trade-offs relating to lawn edges and attic rooms. To the disciplined disposal of garbage and toothpaste stains. To a more discreet attitude to what might be described as soiled footwear and used underwear. And who was it that played cricket with the son of the breeder on Saturday mornings? Not your father. He was in Honolulu or Spain, and cricket's not *my* game.'

'I have nothing to say, Mother, until my lawyer gets home from wherever he is this time.'

'And *who*,' Mother concluded, 'failed to scrub the kitten

stains out of the carpets? And neglects to this day to empty the litter tray, clip the toenails, exterminate the fleas, degunk the ears, medicate the worms and set the corrective mouse traps in the pantry?'

There was no way to win.

Now, thought Knut, if Independence Day ever comes for me personally, I'm going for dogs. Large dogs. We've always been attracted to one another, with our teeth in our pockets and our claws in gloves. Huskies. Alsatians. Borzois. Otterhounds. Pure bred, my friends. Sire secured in one pen; dam disposed in another. Access allowed for fifteen minutes of demanding physical excess under stud-master management on three consecutive days. No wild purple passion in the paddocks. No lusting down the back lanes. Responsible, serious-minded application to the duties of propagation as expected of the cream of species. Then when I'm ready, I'll flick the coin as often as required to eliminate *all but the breed I prefer.*

Do I detect a bleep from outer space?

'Are you expecting, kid, to live a thousand years?'

That couldn't be the voice of God. God wouldn't be so common. A voice that was followed immediately by further bleeps from deeper recesses of space: 'Alleged immatures of your present age, or thereabouts, have married into fortunes. Others have fathered heirs to fortunes. Youths no older than thee have ruled the world. Give thought to that and its calamitous implications. A moment's thought being notably less painful than the reality.'

Might this have been Satan concealed under the left foot of God?

'Take a serious look at yourself, kid. Grit the teeth. Bear the shock. You're the wreck on the rock. Alone on the throne. Forgotten by Mankind. Abandoned by the eye in the sky, and not a comely woman to be seen. Who makes the rules when the maid and the dame and the ruling queen are away at the sales?'

Knut with a leap of illumination.

'I do.'

'Well, pull yourself together and get on with it!'

THE SNOW-WHITE DOG

*Not one more phantom could
Knut hold down.*

Thereupon, Knut felt duty-bound to prise open his eyes.

It proved to be uncommonly beautiful out there; a hazed evening of complex hues infinitely stronger than light. Illumined with shafts of rose, gold, ruby and lilac, as if riches were spilling from the hands of the greedy day as it hastened to make its getaway, leaving Knut to flounder in the spoils, labouring with his images and trying to cope with an extraordinary scene.

His place on the ledge was exactly as it had been. The mountain had not in any way moved; it remained an island in the same world of water. And the same old bones from the same old dead things were lying to his left and his right as before, unchanged, and all manner of questions were volleying and thundering in darkened areas of his brain.

Knut briefly closed his eyes once more, attempting to quieten his thudding heart. Looking again, but sighting a creature that had to be an imagining. Had to be a part of a swelling in his heart.

Now it was not a ghostly leopard in the shadows or the glare.

And it was no serpent or dragon or minotaur out there. Instead, he saw a snow-white dog, glistening, as if groomed with love within the last hour, that ancient breed formed in the wild out of one of Nature's most noble dreams.

Knut was afraid he was seeing through the screen of a wandering mind or through the mists of a thousand years. This dazzling dog of the steppes; how and why could he be here, back straight, head high, in the heat of the evening? The herder of reindeer? The companion and friend of Humankind? The one who warmed the bed? The dog that never ran behind? The ancient breed that drew the sled?

Not one more phantom could Knut hold down.

I thought the samoyed, he said, took you on the run and swept you off your feet. Why's he staying over there looking shy?

Is it that he's young, and here it's strange and in no way like his lovely snow? Might he need another day or two like a day or two of mine to come around? Who would bring a dog like this to me? A samoyed? A sam? Who would have known? Have the gods shown mercy at any other time?

Knut was dragging his words up through solid rock, it seemed: 'Sam, young friend, make the move. You're safe with me. Come to me. Please. Please, Sam.

'Why should I imagine someone like you? Have I seen such a dog in years and years? If we hadn't gone to the Show; if we hadn't met the breeder there; if Mother hadn't said that gorgeous little sam cannot be real, I wouldn't have known what you were.

'Do come on over, my friend. If I crunch through these bones, what will be left when I get to where you are? The dust of all our bones and nothing more?'

Where, thought Knut, are these tears of mine coming from? There must come the tear that'll drain my life away.

'Sam, please, please come.'

Knut pleaded with opened hands and entered a dark country full of fears. 'It is I,' he said, 'who will have to go to you. Oh, do not vanish like the leopard! Stay! Stay. Do not move. I must know you're really there. I must touch you. I must wrap my arms around. Oh, be a living creature! Be alive. I must know I am not alone for evermore.'

Knut was already on his way towards the dog, aware of whispered words somewhere near: 'Lean my way. Lean on me, young man.'

When he came to where the dog sat, Knut placed his hands upon his head and said, 'You're warm. You're real. You're solid. You're Sam.'

At once, another creature, human or a little more, robed in dark brown with a large key on a chain about her neck, offered broken bread, dates and wine. She reminded him of a woman he once saw, glowing in darkness like an icon – who in turn had reminded him of the portrait of Grandmother Mannerheim in Mother's writing-room at the corner of Sebastian and Johann.

After dark, led by Sam, this same creature or person conveyed Knut by one arm across the mountain until they came to a likeness of a door. This opened to the key. In the same order as before, they entered and went underground.

PART THREE
THE KING IS A
THOUSAND
YEARS

REBIRTH AT THE
BREAK OF DAY

*Knut recalls aspects of his life
at home, about Father and
mirrors. He ponders his self, his
wisdom, in this strange state of
limbo or dream ...*

Knut awoke, not knowing from what, to a feeling of well-being, of warm security. He might have been puzzled, a little, but was aware that he belonged to the scene whatever it might have been. A curious feeling, but not off-key. For this, he knew, was the way things were meant to be; as they had been through most of the days he had lived.

Hence it was a feeling that could have belonged to any old Tuesday, Wednesday or Thursday; almost any old day except a holiday. Day-by-day life bearing the stamp of security at the corner of Sebastian and Johann. Though presently Knut's little red numerals, by their absence, were failing to advise him by what margin of time he was ahead or behind, thereby marring a long-established entertainment.

Knut was recalling the guarantee of twenty-five years that accompanied the clock on Christmas morning when he was ten. The same clock was now bidding for the garbage bin with eighteen years of that guarantee, theoretically, left to run.

Not a trace of street light against his window curtains. No movement of traffic. Indeed no window curtains either. Had the Universe gone out of phase during the night and left Knut alone in the dark? Hardly. But it stirred up shadowed memories of dreams relative to firemen, odours, volumes of water and Billingsgate. Along with Father's priceless fire hydrant of 1888 or some other inappropriate date.

It's not, Knut thought, that I'm running late. No one hammers at the door or shrieks up the stairs. I'm in good time and plenty for everything; showering, exercising, breakfast. What can the problem be? The prospect of isometrics in the dark? No mirror to concentrate the striking effects? Do I care? Do I really?

'Pitting one's self against oneself,' Father says, 'is a holy matter in which lies ultimate self-reliance. Stand before the mirror, my son, as stark as the ziggurat on the plain. In your splendour, as God made you. In which I so much enjoyed an immodest hand. How could God mind, having made me in splendour before you? None will spy unless you fail to draw the blind against the bore next door or the eye of the young lady diagonally opposite, occasionally at home. Gorgeous child, Bridget. You must have seen her. You must have noticed.'

Bridget? Who's Bridget, for pity's sake?

Bridget?

'Fearlessly confront the mirror,' Father says. 'Through the ages each mirror has lived with one thought. To greet you eye to eye and navel to navel at break of day. Decline to be diverted by idle self-satisfaction. Nothing's so good it can't be made better. Look what I've done with me.'

Knut becoming more aware of oddly positioned areas of heat

to the rear. Might some person be there? An unlikely idea. Beneath the many-gabled roof of Richard and Madeleine? Each ridge up there petitioning the Heavens: Lord, spare us from the perils of the night, but most especially have mercy upon us, such miserable sinners are we.

Knut's nerves were rocketing towards Judgement Day.

'Nanette!'

But an animal was there instead.

Knut's years went tumbling into the mists. Once his years were reasonable, were real, but no longer, no more. In *this* place, his years were as numerous and as curious as the tales told to her Arabian king by Shahrazad.

In time, the world began again and Knut's shocking awareness of animal heat against his body became as if the Great Lion of the Universe had settled there, for all things were remembered by Knut. Hence his desire was to become fragments of himself. He was like God at the beginning, appalled by eternities of solitude, uttering the Word and fragmenting into Creation in an ever-accelerating escape from Himself.

Knut's instinct was to disconnect, to shed skin, limbs and organs like leaves. Even to be the tiniest of creatures, an insect, an amoeba, with a tiny brush and a vat of ultramarine as big as the world, sentenced to paint all the seas and skies of history. But it was his wisdom not to move a muscle or a nerve. It was his wisdom to draw breath as silently as if he were not there.

Could he flee into darkness away from himself? What might darkness be? Was it a wall, a numbing blow, a pit of spears, a softness enveloping the human frame only to congeal about it like rock?

Why seek to be someone else? Why fall like the leaf? Why paint the skies and the seas? No known exit from the human estate was a certain escape. No one knew what was there.

Knut obeyed his wisdom, making no move, committing no sound, blunting each reckless arrow of thought. So great was the labour that time in this world of his again took on the qualities of millennia and the past became even farther distant and memory turned unreliable and night broke faintly into day and thoughts like germinating seeds began to stir and run away.

All the time, I know I've been heading for this one break of day. But who has planted me here and why?

No well-meaning future, I've heard Father say, hopes to be other than generous, loving, and full of good things. Sadly, futures, like people, are vulnerable and changeable and run into trouble.

I, sighed Knut, am my father's son, born to tedious reflection as one is born to red hair and colour of skin.

He thought of his father considering the break of day: he might part his sticky eyelids and observe, 'Day here again? Couldn't it have asserted itself and stayed at home? What's it doing around here at this hour? Night's good enough for the rest of the world. That's the trouble with this country. Can't pick day from night and doesn't bloody care. For God's sake, I'm seventy-two years old; is it never to mean anything to be venerable? What responsible day would come busting in here without a pot of coffee and a revealing neckline?'

Mother, on the other hand, dealing with the dawn: 'Hearken unto the clatter in the East as of china fragmenting in the dish-washer. Up cometh the glorious day. Out of there; attend to nature's imperious calls. Put on thy little woolly pants and thy little woolly hat. Grab thy skis and let's get the hell out of here.'

Knut was making a mighty effort to find something of himself, to put aside diversions that belonged to the lives of others, even his parents. It's difficult, he said, they're my space suit. I must buckle them on from time to time. Whereupon, he measured the faint growth of light in the sky, translating it into the urgency: what was it that threatened from behind?

Knut went on steadying himself, and slowly, invisibly, bracing himself and pressing up to a sitting position, hands to a surface that was unyielding, unfamiliar, almost level, providing no clues for his nerve ends; then creeping the fingertips of his cold left hand farther and farther around into shocking contact.

A large-headed creature, maned like a lion, almost frightened him witless, but instantly dogs were everywhere. Thudding against his back. Leaping into his arms. Bowling him over. Resolving into one joyous creature, SAM, and one overwhelmed young man.

Not a word was spoken. Not a sound.

His sire is a mountain, but he's my *hound. Mother can't show* him *the door. The key is in my hand.*

Knut's face was at last receiving the tongues of the one thousand daydreams of his very own dog of long ago.

Shortly, Knut and Sam settled side by side, establishing their contract, anxious to get everything right. But Knut was deeply troubled by questions. Sam might have known the answers if he had heard the questions. Knut saw that as the tragedy of the moment; a friend with whom he would never be able to communicate at a level of substance.

So dog and young man sat in that curious non-night and non-day, getting to know each other as well as they were able. No knowing or saying, at that time, what it meant for Sam. Even for Knut there were questions; a great many, and becoming more. For this was the young dog he had called Sam; the one upon whose head he had placed his hand. Thus causing new spaces to open in the world.

Knut said, 'Sam; I observe that you are quite grown up. No mere lad any more. So what of me?'

Eventually, Knut went on. 'Now what am I supposed to think of the smudges out there? They widen but have no golden edges like dawn. No beginnings that I can see and no endings. What is it but a darkness that has stopped being dark but declines to turn into light. How am I to know if it's daybreak or not; if it's one of ours or belongs to somewhere else?

'For the present, Sam, all I wish for us is a safe place in the dark. I'm not sure I want to see any more just yet. True, I can't see you in the dark, as beautiful as you must be, but I know that you're there. And I know you're beautiful even if in truth you turn out to be as ugly as a barn door.

'Am I to deduce from this that yesterday's yesterdays lasted through years? What of the ledge where I wish never to find myself again? Between then and now there is an emptiness, thank God. That high, rugged place I remember as a form of giddiness felt long ago. I have no memory of what lies between. Between the now and the long ago. But am I hungry or thirsty or emaciated or in need? No.

And, Sam, I have you.

...

154

SON OF RICHARD Canute and Madeleine Mannerheim, you have come to an edge.

Nothing is made by Mankind, but Mankind is free to manipulate and initiate change. This was foreseen. This, gladly, was granted as soon as Mankind emerged.

First steps have been on offer to you. As to others. As to all who are able to discern, any such step would have brought you this far with less effort and pain. The pain of your coming this far was not foreseen, but too many choices granted to you have not been perceived by you. THE END, young man, in relation to you, may begin to mean what it means. Take care. Take care.

Limbo is not a judgement or a punishment. You invent it for yourself. You inflict it upon yourself. It is a waste and a sadness for everyone who watches, for everyone left behind, for those who love you and watch over you from a distance; who love you; who love you. Do try to understand.

Knut said to Sam, 'I hear voices. People get put away for less. Am I straying in and out of their wavelengths? Am I picking up thoughts from someone else? From the one reading the report; the one seeing the show; the one who's paid the money and sits in the back row. When the last reel ends and he goes home, what happens to me?

'Things begin to fit my old recurring dream. This worried kid I see in London Town. Dressed for long ago. Pasty-faced. Matted hair. In need of clothes and a shave and self-care. As a mischievous mirror might well remind me. The kid isn't all of me, but he's part of me.

'He's dumped on this London street. Doesn't know why or

how. Says he's from Sebastian and Johann. No one's heard of Sebastian and Johann. I alone know that Sebastian's my nature and Johann is my back gate. The kid tells them that the people of Sebastian and Johann are fifty thousand years old! He doesn't explain why he's younger himself. Doesn't say why he's pasty and uncared for. But he walks the same street in the same dream so often dreamt, always wondering why – long, long before he reaches the mountain where he's conceived.

'I wake up with pounding heart. Taking in gulps of air. I go down the back stairs and drink milk.

'Sam . . . In dreams we don't tell ourselves we're dreaming. We are unaware there's another place called reality. I'm not wrapped in this idea of limbo. I don't see myself as a spook with too much on my mind. Sam, are we helpless spooks together or have you been shanghaied, too? What infamies do samoyeds commit? I suppose there could be a few.

'One step, two steps, three steps ahead, my friend, may settle it for me and for you.'

Knut went down on one knee, labouring against a sudden shortage of breath, hugging his Sam, hoping for answers, reaching only an explosion of resentment. Coming out of it with a mindless charging into darkness; ignoring all instinct of danger; sweeping shockingly onto a slippery slope as long and as steep as a speedway, sending him shrieking into insecurity, clutching at his dog to break the fall, but reprimanded severely and subliminally from within:

Let the dog go.

CRYSTAL OF TIME

Knut discovers the waters
surrounding the mountain upon
which he awakes, and first
encounters the massive form
of the ziggurat.

Knut felt that he had been caught up in a rogue but daring crystal of time, separate from all others; from the world of long ago; even from the unseen world of the long night in the mountain, and of now.

Suddenly, Knut was hearing water fracturing about him like breaking glass, taking its impact through his shins.

What is this, he thought? What now?

It was real, live, living, forgiving water; as if he had plunged into a warm tub out of doors in the balmy night air, with body and head and hair all at length streaming behind. He had an instant sense of healing and of forgiveness for his foolishness; an instant realisation that he had plunged from the side of his mountain into the waters that lay around and below.

Knut sensing their depth and singing songs to springtime and to love and to buds on the bough. Vowing kindness to elderly ladies. Courtesy to old gentlemen. Consideration to babies. Devotion to dogs. Patience with parents, constancy to the less discouraging gods and eternal love for his darling Nanette, come what may.

'Oh, thank you, thank you, my beautiful people up there, my lovely old-fashioned gods prancing on your unicorns, reclining on your clouds, supping on your grapes, having a high old time. When you come to grips with the job, what miracles you perform! Which button did you press? Who wrote the program?

'But I note the usual sting in the tail. For reasons known only to you, suddenly you leave me welded by the feet to the mud at the bottom. I don't call that a fair go.'

Knut wrenching his feet free, almost in desperation; turning himself into a bubble, breaking the surface and bellowing: 'Sam! Don't you hear the ringing of the phone?'

To which Sam responded in the manner given to dogs in wait of a call.

'Over here!' Knut shrieked. 'Come on, come on, you gorgeous beastie; let's see what there is of you.'

Knut headed into a greater orbit of ecstasy. 'We're alive as in Alive! Knut & Sam Proprietary Limited, Manufacturers of Mutual Satisfaction.

'Genuine antique H_2O. And as they have no need of it in Heaven (except to water the wine) and a conservation problem in Hell, I conclude that our company HQ is lodged on Earth where water comes fit, fresh, feeble, foul or fragrant and most heavily on Sundays when it should be fine.

'Oh, real live living water gathered from Heaven in baskets woven by hand for Knut and Sam by the Trade Guild for the Perpetuation of Canines and their Custodians.

'But was this everything my chaplain ever taught me? "Entertain no heresies," said he, "especially a sense of enquiry.

Stick your head in a bag. Carry the bag at all times and generously support the clergy."

'Sire, how could you not have noted my scrupulous attention to the maintenance of the bag? Never a word of protest from me. Never a doubt. Never calling You by nasty names. I retained for personal use only a few modest profanities and my escape clause as guaranteed under the hire purchase act of AD 1215 bearing the name Magna Carta and the signature of King John.

'Real live living water is showering all around me like blessings from above. A question, Sire; where in Hell did *all* this water come from? A question at once modified with apologetic beatings of the brow on the nearest concrete balustrade. Oh, what merriment, what revelry; the beating of oneself brainless for Thee!'

Knut, in the delirium of his reprieve, was waltzing in the water, in the certainty that it was there, confirming it had been there all the time, that it was here and all around, that the mountain was an island in the midst of a sea, or a lake, or a flood as great as any that had ever been. Though in a lightening world of grey upon grey, Knut failed to observe Sam's distress, mistaking it for play.

Knut, instead, became aware of a massive building looming in the mists, a construction almost inconceivably large, stepped up level upon level, each level of great magnitude and of a kind that could have borne the signature: Richard Canute, architect.

Gone, in an instant, was Knut's sweetness of elation and his wild, wild freedom. Instead, into his mind the Matterhorns came back with the Mannerheims, and the later Canutes came back with their obsession to obligation and duty. Knut, greatly burdened, sought an interval of escape, and took down with him into the depths a draught of air that could never have come from the foot of any Matterhorn approved by Grandmother; faintly sour and distinctly warm. It drove him back up in seconds to a surface world dominated by the desperations and screams of Sam which were more than Knut's nerves were intended to stand.

'Idiot bloody Sam! You're not abandoned. Come when you're called.'

Sam went on screaming and Knut, fractiously, feverishly, went after him and grabbed him by a handful of hair.

'Bloody fool of a dog. Bloody pussy-cat of a dog. Dogs save people and dogs paddle them ashore. Not the other way round.'

Sam was enveloping Knut, bearing him down, clawing over his shoulders and head, compelling him to burst out from beneath. Knut, in a rage, was swinging a long left arm and turning it into a stranglehold, only to be stricken by a voice from the past, the voice of the lady who knew about dogs, especially samoyeds.

He's no water spaniel, dear. No swimmer, no. He's dressed for the snow. He drowns.

'Sam, I swear I'd forgotten. Hang on hard, Sam. I'd forgotten. I'd forgotten. You're safe now, Sam. It's your Knut, your guardian, your slave. But you're not listening, are you, you stupid bloody dog? You're dragging me down again! All the dogs in the world and I'm lumbered with a stupid samoyed!'

Knut and Sam linked by limbs, hands and hair . . .

Knut was supporting himself on paddlewheels, or so it seemed, and the buoyancy of all the sour air he could stand. He was encircled by water that he knew to be metres deep, by water and mist. No view of his Matterhorn now. No trace of the great building. If there at all, the movement of the mists had obscured it.

Knut's mood was a confusion, a sickness, a hollowness, a lightness, a heaviness, an anxiety of distractions and spasms of inappropriate foolishness. Telling himself he was not disturbed by the length or breadth or depth of these waters. Had he not swum the English Channel in the swimming pool of a cross-Channel ferry?

'Yesterday,' Knut said to Sam, 'we were dying for a lick. Yesterday we were dehydrated. That's if yesterday was yesterday and not last year. The world, of course, is bloody mad. Feast or famine; flood or fire; sweet or sour; it can stuff itself, I say, full of yesterday's yesterdays. Today I've gone carnivorous again. All this water means waterhen. Means eggs, fertile and fresh. I couldn't care less and couldn't care which. Give me a spear and a loincloth and gravy on my chin and I'll dance in the fire.

'Two eggs and heaped-up potatoes with diced onion. Fried. Four slices of hot toast. Buttered. Unaccompanied by healthful fruit of any description. If you broke me down, Sam, into components, you'd find banana skins, orange rind, apple cores, half-digested pears and bits and spits and pips and peel. I *lust* after fat to be washed from my jowls with black coffee and coddled cream.

'But what do I get? A Matterhorn I can't see, a dog so dumb he was born to drown and gutfuls of stale air.' At which point, Knut yelled, 'I've stood all I'm standing!' And a turbulence moved the mist, and the lower levels of his Matterhorn, of the great building, came again into view.

'There it is! As I knew it would be. But is it moving, Sam? Is it self-propelled? Is it farther away?'

Knut, ritualistically, raised his eyes to the first level of the ziggurat, then to greater levels, three times ascending, until nothing but the lowering sky was left to consider; as remembered with rainbows from another time and a higher viewpoint.

'*My* Matterhorn,' Knut said, whether aloud or not he had no idea, 'proves to be a subject with which I am not unfamiliar. Bear with me, Sam. You're not likely to drown. Strategically, I'm underneath you.

'Theoretically, we're confronting Father's fundamental mass. Essential knowledge for any dog of mine. There can be nothing like this contraption standing between here or anywhere else on planet Earth or we'd *never* have had Father at home. He'd have given an arm and a leg for a sight of it. I detect the stirring of a Force 10 wind sweeping through the Institute of Architects. Sam, I hear from the crypt of the British Museum a clamour among the artefacts and a rattling among the Babylonian bones.

'Or has my little mind gone off like a firecracker? Am I painting my own rainbows and building my own ziggurats? Could a ziggurat stand fair and square in this state of repair through two hundred generations? This, dear Sam, is the greatest ziggurat of all.

'Father's modest fundamental mass in the middle of town back home is constructed from concrete, steel and glass, with foundations on rock. This has got to be mud brick, maybe baked, maybe not, and standing high and dry and apparently in good repair in the midst of a lake or a sea.

'Four levels are visible to me, but *seven* there'll be altogether, with my lovely Oxford leathers stuck in the mud on one level or another lower down! My regrets, Mother dear, but better by far it should be they than me.

'So, dear Sam, I'm the dolphin and you're the lucky lad. Be still, my friend; hang on hard. Make it as easy for your dolphin as you can. For a problem becomes apparent. The farther I swim, the more we are behind.'

Knut sighed from a great sadness that was growing within him.

'It's not a lake, Sam, into which we have so foolishly sprung. Not a sea either, I'm afraid. We can't look forward to a turning of the tide to carry us back to the ziggurat. And a dog as smart as you must know that one free arm to swim with won't do when water is flowing downhill.

'It's a bloody great river, Sam. No knowing where it's come from and no knowing where it's going. No knowing how far away the river banks might be. No knowing. Buckle your belt, my friend. Gird your loins. I need two arms to survive.'

THE MAGICAL, MYSTICAL, AMAZING HAND OF WOMAN AND MAN

Knut is told about the lady of the dogs, and of the contract between human and dog.

WELL, KNUT, THERE was this lady of the animals. She knew about dogs. All dogs. She knew the mind of a dog almost as well as her own.

Knut said: I know, I know.

The lady knew especially about samoyeds. She bred them, raised them, and from her kennels they went out into the world. It was with respect that her friends called her 'Ma'am'.

I know, I know, Knut said. But don't strike me with conscience now. One arm to swim by in a current like this? Don't be absurd. I must have two or I'll drown.

She was a lady whose opinions and judgements were sought in distant lands, who held her dogs by the paw when they were young or sick or scared. Fear was not an uncommon state of mind among healthy sams. Like healthy humans, they used their imaginations. She piped music into their kennels when they were lonely or disturbed and sat with them through the night when their babies were born. And at life's end, she'd bury them with respect and grief and pain.

Knut, you were thirteen.

Knut said: I know. I know I was thirteen. Am I likely to forget the day? Getting dragged away. Leaving the puppy behind.

Your mother was with you and she was forty-eight. Old enough to take to heart what she heard.

Knut said: But she didn't, did she?

Perhaps she took it to heart the wrong way.

'It's for the dog,' the lady said, 'to obey all reasonable commands in good humour and with dignity. The dog is the dog. Never forget what your humanity means to the dog who lives with you. You're his high priest and his god.'

She meant it, Knut, for you to grow up on, though others might have said that your mother troubled her.

The lady, generalising, went on to say: 'It's for the dog to do as you command, even when it wrecks his own agenda. The soft and sensitive person who seriously questions the fairness of this must not forget that the dog was born to it and is required to understand. It's a contract that he sees confirmed each day in the print of his paw and the magical, mystical, masterful movements of your amazing hand.

'He knows the contract is as it stands. If he fails to honour it, he's a rogue. There's no place for a rogue among dogs.

'More than any other creature, he knows that his purpose in life, his fulfilment and crown, is to be the companion, supporter and protector of woman, child and man. In return, he'll look to his human to attend to the several tasks he's unable with dignity to perform. And the human, whilst continuing to enjoy health and strength, must meet these expectations. Not all dogs will expect the same. The expectations of your dog are determined by you.

'Each human taking on a dog, takes on a contract. A loaded contract is null and void. A contract with a dog is not to be entered into unless the intention of the human is honourable; especially if the human is a child. Care and constancy towards the dog may be too much for the child. All too soon the pup is full-grown and the love he holds for the child may far exceed what the child feels for him when playtime's over and school begins.

'Never let the dog know that his contract has swung out of balance. In absolute terms an obvious imbalance is the ultimate tragedy in the life of a dog. Even a passing imbalance is a reality of which he should not be made aware, unless he has offended abominably. This may be his nature occasionally, as it is yours. The sam is a breed with spirit, with roots in antiquity, with a sense of humour, with a point of view and a will of his own.

'."They tell me," he says, "that I am the most beautiful dog in the world. I remain as Nature fashioned me long ago. I came in out of the cold to be with you. But beware; I, alone among dogs, love every woman, child and man simultaneously. I was not made to be deceived, caged or humiliated. I will not scratch at your door. If you fail me, wire will not hold me. The world is full of humans in need." '

The lady said: 'Respect this noble creature when he puts an opposite point of view. If it is inappropriate, he must be told. But never hit him with the hand that feeds him. If he uproots your precious plant, paddle him with the plant. This he'll

166

attribute to your human ways. But if he ceases to respect you, he's not the dog to have around. Allow him to give his love to someone else.

'Throughout his life, he'll bow to a point of order, as the gentleman bows in the presence of a king or queen. It's a bow to tradition, to the way things have been.

'He'll sweep to the ground with style, signalling his willingness to come. Yet know that tomorrow he'll try again. Each time he confronts a fair refusal he'll respond with his bow and consider the dispute, for the moment, at an end.

'A dog is a dog. It's a profound contract, related to our own with the gods.

'In the balance, I believe humans acquit themselves better than the gods. If you fear you cannot meet the standard, never take a dog home. Never, for a moment, consider a sam.'

In a second or two, there it all was: the tale of the magical, mystical, amazing hand.

There it had come and gone, like an orchestra of a hundred instruments committed to a single sound: the voice of the lady of the animals, of the lady they called 'Ma'am', speaking to Mother and looking at Knut from time to time, on the day when Mother had drawn Knut away without the puppy, the longed-for puppy nine weeks old.

Knut had recorded it way back then at the kennels for instant replay now.

THE ZIGGURAT

*Knut confronts the splendid
vision of the ziggurat and
questions why it fills his
world.*

Knut came up out of the waters long afterwards; a half-day afterwards. He came crawling from the great river onto the ziggurat, onto a shelf or step, dragging his dog after him.

Knut's reward was the solid reality of the ziggurat, the knowing that the world as he saw it was as real as he was himself. Knowing and understanding that he had prevailed against an enormous force, that his battle with the waters left him in debt to no one, human, animal or god.

He had honoured, as if to the death, the value of the life of this beautiful creature that he scarcely knew, and his vow to the God he was seriously beginning to doubt.

And he had honoured his own understanding of the encounter with the lady of the animals and from whom in anguished disappointment, long ago, he had walked away, hearing Mother say: 'No, no. No, no. The lady did not consider you were ready to take care of a samoyed.' Which Knut had always known was not true.

At last that brooding wound, suffered since boyhood, was

healed. Worthily, he had preserved the life of a creature that he believed to be linked to his own. Worthily he bore new wounds and new pains to remind him; Knut not having attained greatness before, except in odd moments, none of which he remembered. But he had put right the foolish error that had taken the dog with him into the water; an error of a kind he would strive never to repeat.

And he had delivered himself and his dog, each from death, without assistance of any kind. This was his awesome understanding as he grounded on a step of the ziggurat, wide enough to accommodate him at length; seen from the waters as a form of landing stage; the only safe place in the visible world. His numbed right arm encountered it below the surface and in some unremembered way, he manoeuvred himself a few steps higher before releasing Sam from his locked left side.

The sun by then was almost high and Time required of Knut its portion of flesh and respect. Without remission, Time pressed a hand upon the mere human on the step.

It's not for humans, Time said, to exceed the mortal measure in this manner. Be damned to you. If you would live like a god, suffer like one. Who would be a god who could be mortal?

Consciousness began to stir again through Knut at an hour beyond noon, but an hour of high heat. There was an idea surfacing within him that he had crawled onto this structure around the lower reaches of its second or third level. Other levels were not visible to him. Visible only was the shape of the central stairway on which he had grounded. It was reaching on and beyond him, going up and up and up in a manner odd enough to furnish a dream; a conception splendid enough even to enhance this prince among ziggurats.

Knut went on searching the echoes of his mind, but found nothing there large enough or striking enough to match this ziggurat. No reports or rumours of it. No sketches of it in the memoirs of nineteenth century travellers. Was it an uncelebrated wonder of the ancient world?

Yet memories were beginning to trouble the spirit of the young Knut Canute. Once only had he seen anything similar; a vision of a remarkable structure drafted exquisitely upon a broad sheet of acid-free paper in his father's den at the corner of Sebastian and Johann.

In that private place, Father shaped his gifts to posterity. There they were secure from the ridicule of colleagues and critics, but bared before Knut, whose excitement it was at special times to follow the development of architectural ideas that the world, as it was, would never see. A stairway was observed then in the manner of the stairway here, recessed between two glistening ramps surfaced with tiles the colour of red earth.

A likeness indeed!

So Father *did* have knowledge of this structure! Of what it was and possibly of where it was. Or, had two great designers born thousands of years apart, Father and some person unknown, come up with the same idea?

A daunting spectacle, this stairway upon which Knut stood, soaring from the waters with diminishing detail towards the heat-hazed sky. Built by which extraordinary king of the ancient world? Constructed by legions of artisans or brutalised slaves? By a nation or a continent in captivity? Or by magical manipulation of natural laws?

170

So this was the structure that Knut, on impulse, had abandoned before darkness had turned into day. From somewhere near by he had rushed onto one ramp or the other and shot from its edge into the waters below!

If so, by what means had his mountain become a ziggurat? Or by what means and by whom had he been transferred? Aloud, Knut cried, '*From where has it come and why is it in my world?*'

Ultimately, this was an unstable world, little doubt. With water flowing around and beneath, constantly undermining the superstructure, no matter how hallowed or ancient. Time was the revolving door, the enemy with faces beyond number.

In Knut's mind, his disapproval of Master Time's morality went on growing. Had anyone ever said that *Time*, captain of logic, was captain of himself? What was he but a tool? Or a fool?

'Some mere human,' thought Knut, 'with time to kill, put you together, mate; out of time left over from doing something useful like building a boat or frying an egg or counting the cars through the crossroads. God almighty, half the gods of the Universe are *clay*. Stick 'em in this river and they'd wash away. Or are *you* the river, Master Time?'

Knut moved himself, sternly, to the step immediately above.

'Well, the top's up there and made to reach. We'll get there, one step at a time. Someone's got to be top of the heap. Someone's got to be Hillary and Tenzing.'

Knut had not leapt to this next step, just the same. First, he gathered the grit and fired up the muscle. These steps might have been higher than steps usually were. So Knut sat on the edge, chin cupped in one hand . . .

'Good God! I've got a beard!'

He put two hands to his face, all Hell beginning to burn inside! And somewhere or other someone said: 'Out here where the action is, we abhor foolishness and rage but honour anger. Anger is the fuel we burn.'

Knut's reaction to anger? 'What the bloody Hell! A bloody beard! I call that dirty pool.' This he followed by more hesitations of uncertain length and further outbursts of indignation. Then a severe and deliberate setting-out in a measured manner to mount the stairway, accumulating statistics along the way.

Yellowish steps. Brownish steps. Shortish. Long. Convex. Concave. All as hot as Hell underfoot and so on. Steps of kinds so numerous he lost track of his classifications. Or were the variations subtle enough to be builders' deviations? Due to compromises in the pursuit of profit or problems of supply? To some sly character in an expensive loincloth and a priest's hat, building a shack back in the sticks for wild weekends with the novices? Which reduced the authority of Knut's figures.

To Hell with steps, anyway. He proceeded to classify *pauses*. Once a statistician, always a statistician. His pauses were almost as diverse as the nature of motor vehicles at crossroads.

Pauses for breath. For reflection. For looking around. For thudding the right fist into the left palm. For wrapping the left palm across and around and over his chin to pull at the beard. It looked fiery. It looked red. Along with pauses of no purpose except to express his exasperation with the failure of his statistics to make sense.

Oh, to Hell with pauses.

Status quo.

Who could say what was really *there*? As soon as one made up one's mind, the scene changed. Little doubt about the sun, though, beating down. Unless this were a planet elsewhere. The 'sun' might then be known as 'carousel' or 'Aladdin's lamp' or 'fried egg'.

To Hell with statistics! Who cares?

There was nothing to see but walls to the left and right and steps going up and the same steps going back down. Fiendish. An image that looked more and more like Father all the time. Never a nice old-fashioned observation platform with safety-rail and tourist guide with inset brass arrows: 5 k's to Krakatoa: 50 k's to the Great Fire of London: 500 k's to Pompeii: 5000 k's to Noah's Ark: 5,000,000,000 k's to the Big Bang. And at the top, sky. At the bottom, water. At the centre, the horizon between walls, with the sky remaining stranded for ever up on top, and the water permanently installed below. Knut was halfway up.

Oh, to Hell with observation platforms and tourist guides! But why a structure of this size without rhyme, logic, statistics, status quo or a single bloody brass arrow?

All at once then, Knut could hear the voice of Father in a distant wilderness, Knut not knowing where: *The logic is the structure. The structure is the reason. The rationality is you. Look for the architectural solution.*

Trust bloody Father.

To Hell with everything. Notably the beard.

'I was always going to be clean-shaven! Bloody beard! Bloody nerve!'

Knut experienced a lightening of the head. It was such a long way down; such an outrageous distance; as if with each step he teetered at the edge of some new cliff; each new step testing him again; stretching him again; every few steps seeming marginally higher; marginally deeper; marginally longer. Yes or no? Extraordinary. Am I going to get away up there or shall I come to a step that's too high? That's so bloody high I can't even make it?

I could never, he thought, in a month of pie-eyed Sundays in the clubhouse, take a parachute jump while the plane was airworthy and the pilot wasn't dead. They must be bloody mad.

That lightness of the head was constantly threatening to turn to giddiness, accenting the aches in his calves, the pains in his thighs and the distress of heat felt through his feet. Such elegant feet, Mother once said. Almost feminine, she said. The witch.

Fried feet. Le speciality of le house. Pied a la ziggurat; sauce au piment. The alternative? You won't be catching me sitting on it! thought Knut. No well done middle-loin chops around here.

Come to think of it, there was a time I had a large, white, woolly object under one armpit? Hanging on like I owed him a favour as well as a couple of grand. Didn't I, on his behalf, damn near drown myself to death? A dog built like a carthorse. Bred to pull a truck. Why isn't he pulling me? In his time of need he had a human to hold him up. In my time of need I get nothing but a depressing commentary on the nature of Man's best friend.

Here I am, climbing this bloody great mountain freehand. No ski lift. No funicular. No piggyback. No crutches. Not a push behind and not a sled dog in sniff, snort or sight. And a bloody beard to boot.

Where is that rotten dog?

'SAM!'

Sam, indeed, was a dog again, a working model again, and long ago had bounded up the stairs until, at a point not observed, he shook himself with gusto, spraying all around, very noisily. Silence not being an accomplishment of sams.

Then he bounded down again, but with especial care where the ziggurat ended and the water began, as if it might open up a second time and swallow him down. Then standing over his man and kissing his cheek. Even watching over him for an hour or two, while he groomed his own feet and stretched or made a play bow or walked around or took a little nap or cried, 'Hurrah for lovely dry land. And hurrah hurrah for my adorable guy whose wish is my command if there's not too much else on my mind. Haven't I been waiting on his call since I was two months old and he was thirteen years, with bags under his eyes, in tears, getting dragged away from me by that mother of his? While my lovely lady, the one they all called 'Ma'am', said to me, 'I wanted that boy for you. He was right for you. He'd have grown to be your very own lovely man. I'm sorry, little one. I'm sad.' And so was I. But now here he lies. I've travelled the ages, I believe, through space and time to be with him and when I kiss him he doesn't blink or turn away or scream BLOODY NO. Perhaps he's tired.

If I got kissed by a woolly white dog as beautiful as me, I'd run a mile, kicking my heels, clapping my paws, dragging my latterlies through the snow.

Whereupon, Sam bounded off again, up again and away. Knut knew none of it, lying as he was several steps above the waterline all those hours ago, after he had come ashore from his monumental battle against flood and tide, an outcome of the deluge that began in the twenty-second century AD and continued for seven hundred years.

...

Now Knut said at around the halfway mark of his climb up the ziggurat: 'This isn't the place to stop. I need to keep going. I must not start thinking about what comes next. If I lose my nerve now, what will I do with myself? What is here but me and all the way down and the rest of the way up? Yet I've got this far or I wouldn't *be* this far, though I know it's not prudent to look closely at that.

'SAAAAMMM!'

Has he ever answered to Sam?

He's no pup. He might have been when I was thirteen. But when was all that? Today he's five or six or more. Or that's what he looks. What's he been answering to in the years between? Might his name have been Rover or Nikolai or Prince or Wupp?

Why should *Sam* strike a chord?

Fifty million names out there and only one will bring him running.

How long will it take me to call fifty million names in alphabetical order?

CHAPTER THIRTY-ONE

HIS HOLY INDIGNATION:
HIS RIGHTEOUS ANGER

*I might be your victim. I'll not
be your slave.*

Knut came almost to the top of the great ziggurat. Perhaps six
or seven steps more to go. Each step an absurdity; a stretch, a
strain, an anxiety; each step, hip high.

Knut was unable to relate these distances to reality. Fatigued
and uneasy, he was unable to judge competently the effort he
had expended or the effort he might still be required to find.

His fatigue taking the form of a barrier that said *no*. Surely,
surely, he could have gathered himself and crossed the line in a
few moments into the next unknown. Perhaps if Sam had been
alongside. But of Sam there was still no sign.

An immense world of discoloured water lay far, far below,
unmarked but for the faintly rippled lanes of currents and
breezes and unknown irregularities. No element of life as he
knew it was visible, on the surface, above it or beneath. Now he
knew it was not a lake, not a sea, and now he knew it was not
a river either, but the draining of an area of flooded land of
unknown magnitude. Knut seriously feared it might be the
draining of the planet, wondering if he were observing the cur-
vature of the planet with the naked eye, as if he'd come not to

the peak of a ziggurat, but to the peak of an immensely high mountain. Yet he knew he had climbed fewer than a thousand steps in a direct line, as severe, as challenging as those steps, progressively, had become.

Aloud, he said: 'Who am I to be put to this test? Why should I climb Jacob's Ladder? Was Jacob asked to climb it? Never. The ladder was the symbol of the certainty that God was with him. It was a ladder in a dream. My ladder is no dream and its rungs are too far apart to climb!'

Knut daring to sit at the edge of the step he had reached; but heavily; there to give thought to what he saw; to the problems it raised or concealed.

'Water,' Knut said, 'in all directions open to the eye. Are all other directions the same? Why not? Why not?'

North, south, east, west? In which hemisphere am I, or do I squat on the Equator of this world?

It's a world with one feature, it seems: a ziggurat sited above the level of the father of all the floods that ever have been. Might this ziggurat be the ark? Am I a Noah in disguise?

Then a voice stirred in the midst of his questions. An extraordinary recall:

AUNT INGRID!

'Don't build a thesis, my dear, as big as life, on first impressions. They lead you up the garden path. Take a serious look at what first impressions have done to me. And I was such a bright young thing. Such a pretty young thing. You'd never believe, Darling Knut, you'd never believe.'

Dear, dear Aunt Ingrid. Long ago, with Knut, aged fourteen or fifteen; when in the last hour they had missed the last train home.

The weather-beaten night of the exhibition of artefacts. Iron Age. Bronze Age. Stone Age. And of Ages uncertain. The occasion of the lecture that did not occur, but did not come to nothing.

'Phillip Hann is well known in England,' Aunt Ingrid assured Mother in Knut's hearing, 'even if less known here. I have a personal invitation to this exciting event. I'm familiar with his work in Iraq. A most interesting man. His films are remarkable. An opportunity, dear, for Knut. I really can't go all that way on my own. And archaeology's not Sophie's interest, in the way that it's mine, as you know.'

The Anglers' Hall. Seating arrangements for a modest twenty-eight. A small meeting-place on a dark side street, a disconcerting distance by rail from town. An unlikely venue for an authority on any subject. The more so when it was clear that Hann had arrived independently with his exhibits and only Aunt Ingrid and Knut were there.

'Don't go up front,' Aunt Ingrid whispered. 'Not yet, dear. No.' She settled for the third row.

Hann, arms folded, nodded from a bentwood chair, apparently not phased by his failure to draw an audience other than two, one a mere boy.

Knut was remembering a movement of his shoulders. A sigh. And recalled paintings by Hieronymus Bosch. Hann, Aunt Ingrid said later, reminded her of a koala. At his left elbow was a rough-timbered heavy table, about two metres by one, barely above knee height, displaying a variety of objects of classic form and exquisite craftsmanship, many of which, Knut felt, should not have been removed from controlled atmospheres.

To Hann's right, a kitchen servery opened onto the main room. There a platter of sandwiches, a wedge of crumbling cheese with cheese knife, three dessert plates, a carton of whole milk, three domestic mugs, and a percolating ceramic pot of coffee. No sugar, spoons or adornments. None needed.

Outside, it was a wild night.

What of the organisers and other interested parties? Put off by the weather? Hann, supposedly, had come halfway round the world; Aunt Ingrid and Knut twenty-five kilometres by train; grotesque.

The silence continuing through an uncertain and troubled time. Rain on the roof becoming a roar. Their host said, 'Coffee. Join me, please.'

The organisation promoting the event? *Times: Ancient and Modern*. Knut checked afterwards. *Times: Ancient and Modern* was not listed. But having checked it, Knut shrugged it off.

'These precious and priceless objects, young man, are my property and in my care. They have been for many years. Do not be concerned for their conservation.'

Had Knut put the question? No.

The objects bore striking qualities in common. Inventiveness, singularity and relevance to daily life; excellence of craftsmanship and materials; even a fascinating device for the hand to make fire. 'Handle it if you wish,' Hann said.

'No, sir. Thank you. Thank you. It must be very old.'

'To the contrary. And does it need to be? In a continuing Universe are several thousand years of much account? A single lifetime may stretch our understanding when we're faced with the challenge of living it. Wouldn't you agree? Have you not observed the lives of the adults who cross your path daily?'

'Carbon 14 dating, sir?'

'No. Not relevant nor required.'

As if barely an hour had passed, Knut was hearing Aunt Ingrid's urgent apology and plea: 'As reluctant as I am, sir! It's midnight! We must hurry to catch the train to take us home!'

They ran much of the way. An impressively fit old lady. But the station was locked, in darkness, and was three stops only from the end of the line. Rain fell heavily. The umbrella blew out. The public telephone proved to be vandalised and the guys with the bricks and the bottles were somewhere around the corner.

'Put that brick down, Knut.'

'No, ma'am. I'm wishing it were a foil.'

No taxi rank either and no bus route that hadn't gone to bed.

'Back to the hall, Aunt Ingrid. Let's go. Let's hurry.'

'No one will be there, Knut.'

'He can call a cab. There was a phone.'

'He's gone, Knut.'

'That's not possible.'

'There's a world that you understand, Knut, and there's another that I know. He's gone.'

Would Mother be about to start worrying? And what of Aunt Sophie? Were not Ingrid and Knut each in good hands? Kilometres apart, Mother and Sophie slept soundly and Father was in Arabia with plans. None was to be told, ever, that Ingrid and Knut clambered onto the station after tracking from a distance down-line to seek shelter from cold, wind, rain and hoodlums.

Knut said, 'We should've made it clear we'd go home separately. Then they'd have done something about it.'

Aunt Ingrid said, 'Madeleine assumes you're with me. Sophie assumes I'm with you. At this hour neither would pick up a phone.'

They took a corner of the waiting-room and held hands. Knut

had loved her all his life but knew nothing of what had made her as she was.

They spoke of eternal things and questioned whether the more engrossing passages of life might happen *outside* of life, among the dreams.

Five hours and fifteen minutes later the station lit up, the gates unlocked, and the first train came through.

At the corner of Sebastian and Johann at six-fifteen, Aunt Ingrid said, 'I'm so grateful for the sharing of this mystery with you. It was all arranged for you. Ponder that in your heart as I ponder it in mine. God's blessings, Knut Canute . . . Durham Road, thank you, Mr Driver.'

Knut on his step, high in the sky, head bowed, swaying from side to side, eyes closed.

Why has it taken so long to remember this?

Dear, dear aunt; truly you're not the one to chart a life by; but here I am and you alone might really know why.

I ask: what's happened to *time?* Look at my hands and feet. At my skin. It's matured. And I have a man's beard and a man's hair. The boy has gone along with the time.

Surely, surely I have emerged from having been put aside. From being locked up. Detained. Nothing about me feels like Peter Pan. By what means other than time can a boy turn into a man? But I'm well, strong and sound. I doubt if ever I lost my mind or there'd be a sign. What I remember, I remember. It's clear. But nothing at all lies between. I've had the big sleep. Again and again I have been put aside, deferred, until my time. But where, how, and for what reason is it now?

I am what I am, but have yet to discover what I am. I must have a duty to perform. Am I to be told of its form? If so, by whom? I'm here because I'm meant to be here. I've said that before. Nothing has happened by chance.

All this is made clear simply by stating it.

Knut was thus preparing himself for the ascent of the last few steps of the ziggurat. Each step was to prove to be an obstacle, to be mounted at a stretch and a strain and a scramble. The crossing of the head of the stairway. The confrontation with the crown of the ziggurat – which was still to be observed.

Knut running his hands through his hair. Inspecting his fingernails showing ragged signs of wear. Buttoning to the neck what was left of his jacket and hammering one fist into the other palm. Was he not bred to look his best at all times?

The mess you'll see is not me. There's nothing I can do at present about the way I am. But do not be deceived.

A rush of blood to the head driving him to the top; the hardening of his nerve barely catching up from behind. His stops and starts. His state of mind. His holy indignation. His righteous anger. The king about to lose his head. A fellow feeling for Charles I and Louis XVI. Felt strongest at the crest. There missing a heartbeat and writing it off. There a step without a scramble or a stumble. Then . . .

Knut confronted a landing; low, even and wide. Over the top without break of stride into an open space; perhaps the forecourt, its perimeters massed with vegetation.

Knut glimpsing even the half visible; words not for speaking aloud coming to mind: Whoever You may be, it's Your doing, not mine. Don't nail me to the tree.

A low table about three metres by one, of rough timbers, barely knee height, stood in his way, sheltered from direct light by a bleached canopy stirring to light air movements. Beyond it, at a distance, there was an opening, a track or trail in the wall of vegetation.

With extraordinary concern, Knut recognised the rough table and the finely crafted objects it bore, but among them were items not seen before. A scabbard and, notably, the unsheathed sword.

Were centuries compacting into moments? Was it an eternity since Knut had climbed the stairs at midnight to bed on July 3–4? The same eternity since the firing squads (if any) had fired, and the trains (if any) had roared through tunnels, and aircraft (if any) had blown up, and rocket vehicles had lifted off to another world? A few score or a few hundred years ago? Or were there millennia lodged in between?

Two long strides short of the table, Knut settled on his age. A moment of revelation. He determined that he was old, but young. Was worn, but new. Was around twenty-two, but all of a thousand. And instantly, barefoot, he came to a guardsman's halt and never felt the pain.

'I might be Your victim. I'll not be Your slave. As You see me, so I am.'

PART FOUR
ZIGGURAT: THE ARCHITECTURAL SOLUTION

STATEMENTS OF
PRINCIPLE AND DESIGN

*Assuredly, Knut seems to be no
one's slave.*

Knut was holding his stand before the rough-hewn table, parade
ground style, cadet corps style.

He was standing to attention there, prepared even to be
struck down from behind, but making no movement other than
with his eyes. If he were to be taken from the rear, so be it. On
Father's authority: 'No glancing back, ever, over the shoulder
when you make a stand on principle. Deny them the satisfaction. I have wished that friends and enemies had drawn their
swords sooner. I have wasted much goodwill on barren ground.'

This table and its display were lying in wait for Knut. Reading
from extreme right to left, there was a silvered sword almost as
fine as a foil, made by a sensitive and knowing hand, its sole
ornamentation a crafted hilt. Sword and scabbard, elegantly
slender, exquisitely long.

'Mine? Well, it's got to be or it wouldn't be here. All comers
be warned of me. I am the green-eyed dragon with thirteen tails.
I strike from all around. But if I were reading the table from the
left instead of from the right, the sword would not come first,
but last. I must keep that in mind. My need of it may not be

critical. Someone may be playing a mean game. *Choose,* this Someone says. *If you make the right choice, well and good. If you make the wrong, drop dead.*

'Father,' said Knut, 'never dilutes a statement of principle or design; but compromise attracts me. I'll read this table from both ends and be ready to leap both ways!'

A voice might have said: *Wise. Wise.*

One plate; two bowls; one platter, and an ingenious device to fit the hand to make fire.

'Mine? It must be, or it wouldn't be here either. Once before I was invited to handle this device. I declined. I do so again. When I need fire I'll choose my own way.'

Of this, a voice might have said: *Interesting. Very. Assuredly, he is no one's slave.*

Next there was one knife, one fork, one spoon, all crafted from silver. Superb. Two matching beakers. Two earthenware jugs of traditional form; glazed; each topped with a square of net weighted with beads. Traditional. One probably containing water; the other possibly wine. Both undoubtedly warm.

A crusty loaf. A netted jar, perhaps of honey. 'No,' Knut said, 'honey is *not* for me.' A block of dates. A block of figs. Pistachio nuts and walnuts lying so carelessly they could only have been arranged. One polished apple of unidentified kind . . .

Finger bowl and hand basin with water, both of white porcelain. A hand-loomed towel, folded. A robust cushion of purple burlap.

Surprise, surprise, thought Knut. I'm pressed to take my ease, but I elect to remain on my feet. An inherited fault that my hosts may understand.

They'll know what I'm thinking, but I must do it my way. All

I will take from here is time to consider my choices. I take nothing for granted or it may fade from view like the eagle, the leopard and Sam.

Next in line on the rough-hewn table was a cotton garment of royal blue; night and day wear, airy, free and easy. Indistinguishable from Mother's purchase in Copenhagen. Folded to accent its two pockets. Over the left pocket the crest, KMC, embroidered from threads drawn from gold.

Knut's heartbeat was beginning to register levels of extreme alertness and extreme discomfort.

Next! Basic sandals, sturdy, to fit the lean foot. A hat, broad-brimmed, the colour of red earth. A brush for vigorous use in the mouth. A metal mirror, colour of steel, pocket sized. Father's voice crossing the years: 'Never flew a mission without that steel mirror in my left breast pocket. The *Iliad* in the right breast pocket. What else for the right-hearted man?'

'You could have tried a Bible,' Knut said.

'Who's bringing up who?'

But here there was no Bible or *Iliad* to deflect weaponry, and Knut's own copies were not to be found at the head of these stairs that he had climbed to the sky. They were elsewhere in space and time.

Then there was a folded umbrella. For shelter from rain? For shade? Frame possibly of split bamboo. Fabric varnished or waxed, colour of pewter, bearing designs folded from view.

A comb; it could have been sliced from tortoiseshell with the sharp edge of a flint or a laser. Beside the comb, a pair of silvered scissors; a length of strong plaited cord looped at one end with silvered clip at the other; a plaited belt with hip-bag attached; the silvered scabbard and the silvered sword.

Knut was resisting each urge to move, feeling like the small boy who feared he had been dumped in a dustbin to die; who'd given way to unworthy thoughts, however justified.

He calmed himself and closed his eyes on everything around. Hence he missed by a second or two the approach of his elegant and stately snow-white dog.

Knut said, often pausing in search of words:

'Father of gods; with what and with whom am I speaking?

'I find myself alive, but scared. It's as if I'd been thrown against walls. I earnestly thank my ancestors for sturdy genes, but look for compassion on the human condition. I wish not to deal exclusively with gods. I have in mind where I might be and say it is time for intentions and realities to be made clear?

'Thank you for the table as set before me. For food. For drink. For material things from which I will choose for right or for wrong. For clothing – as you have dressed the creatures of the wild according to their needs. For means of self-care. For not leaving me defenceless. For the sword to buckle on. Its true edge shall be my own body.'

Knut's sense of solitude was broken only by the pulse beating hard in his head. By winds as heard in high places, by bird calls as in dreams, by animal cries as at nightfall. By sounds of living things getting ready to grow.

'Thank you for the mysteries that have brought me here. And, as of now, I submit, conditionally, to what is required of me in good conscience. If I come to serious question, I may not obey.

'The past that made me as I am has gone. The boy has gone and I did not experience his passing. Give me time now and then to make amends for what I've lost. It's human to be human.'

...

In Knut's own private time, he broke the spell and opened his eyes.

Evening had come.

He said to himself, 'Tin soldier; you've served your stint on the tabletop. Stand at ease!' And at once he saw the huge black eyes of his beautiful sam close to his side, head framed by a hooked leg to the left and a statement from the straight leg at the right.

Good evening, sir.

This coming courteously from Sam, who added: I've kept an eye on you, sir. Upstairs and down. Round and about. But a dog has many calls on his time. Much to keep an eye on, and the smells; a wonder they've not driven you out of your mind.

Knut on his knees, drawing his heavy hands through soft masses of wool. 'Dear Sam.'

Your love makes it a kind of Heaven, sir, Sam said. Life's most wonderful surprise. Even wicked dogs like me know a thing or two that humans fail to understand. If you were not here, I would be dead or not born. You're the call and the cause, sir, and I thank you for carrying me through the waters this day and for bringing me safely to shore. But do give thought to the climate now and then. I'm a snow dog, sir, and appreciate shade from time to time. That stairway had none.

'Sam, my fingers find a rolled collar here . . . I thought sams and collars were not the ideal match . . . '

A vexation, sir, endured since my retirement from the ring. Too boisterous, they said. I'm nobody's nobody, you know. I can throw my weight around. Dog of the Year, all breeds, best in show at the Royal before I turned three. Heady stuff. Now there'll be a hullabaloo and a shaking in the shoes. Some villain's stolen our gorgeous boy to make a rug of him? Better their worry than mine.

Nothing's made up for the day you walked away, sir. Last of the litter. Nobody's baby. All my brothers and sisters had gone to new homes. I wasn't born to be Dog of the Year. I was the runt of the litter. The late starter. It all happened by surprise.

I'll be sticking around, sir, but sometimes out of view in the shade. When you want me, call. When I'm old and hard of hearing, shriek. I'm the king's dog, sir, until I die at your feet. Difficult; the short lives us dogs must bear; though I've come to understand that we're creatures born to suffering and anger and ecstasy and enough's enough, I suppose.

With an arm about his sam, Knut said: 'We've changed, haven't we? Each of us. Change is a process of time, they say. It may take even more time to learn what time has done to us.'

I, sir, well I differ from day to day. A lazy bum on Sundays. I've been known to be a hero on Mondays once or twice. A wimp on Tuesdays; most Tuesdays. Wednesdays we won't discuss. Thursdays, of a consequence, find us in trouble of one or another kind, making Friday the anticlimax every time. Saturday's my day. It was Saturday when we were young and we met for the first time. On Saturday I won the Royal. And today, sir, I'll be joining you at the table. The bowls are mine. I'm very partial, sir, to much of what's there, but regret the absence of scrambled eggs with cheese, sage and thyme.

'I wish,' Knut said, 'I could read your eyes.'

All good things, sir, in good time.

Knut reached for the steel mirror and inspected his own reflection, most seriously and much surprised. 'Well, there's a man,' he said. 'Hello to you, Knut Canute. Where the Hell did you come from?'

The first of Time's dirty deeds, sir. Look what it's done to me. A grandfather over and over and over again.

'That's no boy I see in there,' Knut said.

And I'm no pup, sir, either. Not that I'd wish to be boasting too much about those lovely little girls who used to knock at my door. Not in the course of one wild fling, sir. Enchanting idea, just the same. Each little girl approved by and under my lady's supervision, though the Establishment allows an experienced sire like me to decide for himself. If I feel disinclined, sir, that's it. In the light of recent events, I might've made a hasty decision or two. A mere twenty-nine daughters and thirty-five sons and nothing of interest to a virile sam around here. Not for want of searching, sir, as you may yourself in time confirm.

But first I'd suggest the scissors, sir. I might only be the dog on the mat, but any nice young human lady around here would have fled at the sight of you. Time, sir, to give your whiskers a trim.

'Good God, Sam! The *colour* of my skin!'

Looks fine to me, sir. If you'd come up looking like a crocodile . . .'

'I'm *brown*.'

Masculine, sir. All the rage.

Knut was ripping his hard-worn jacket down the front.

That's some man in there, sir. A real high-class tan.

'Sire, what was wrong with the way I was born?'

Sam's the name, sir. Champion Sabaka Silver Czar. Sab, for short. But Sam'll do. I don't stand on ceremony except at stud. And don't insist on 'sire' except on registration papers. Now what's all this panic about brown? Biscuit colour is in my line, sir, lightly toasted, and much in demand. You can't seriously question a healthy tan.

'Why change me?'

You're not listening, sir, are you?

'Brown all the way up and all the way down.'

If you're brown, sir, you're brown. Peanuts are peanuts and giraffes don't expect to hop around. Humans come blended, sir. Cross a sam with a red setter and you've really got something to knock 'em down.

'Brown as bloody boot polish.'

I'd have said autumnal, sir.

'Bloody genes.'

(Hey nonny nonny, sir, for a never and anon and a neigh.)

'Some bugger's been out on the tiles.'

That's getting rude, sir.

'With a taste for exotica!'

A healthy two-way attraction, sir. Multi-cultural. A principle us dogs have lived by and enjoyed for donkey's years.

'Sam. The table is set. The food is in wait. Let's eat.'

You mean, sir, let's *celebrate*. No doubt about Saturdays, sir. All Saturdays are great, but this one wins the blue ribbon. This one wins the prize.

THE KING ON THE
SCAFFOLD

*In which Knut takes up arms
and confronts the unknown
with Sam.*

'On my life,' said Knut, 'there's no way I can leave this table looking like it's been ravaged by a pack of hooligan dogs.'

Knut apologised with a glance at Sam and a thought, in brief, to the rowdy element at Wittenberg College on the occasion of the last annual class dinner. Knut then proceeded to tidy the table in the manner of his mother before him. A game at which not only gods and women could play. Knut eventually seating himself on the edge of the table, one cheek on, the other off, stubbornly brushing at his very long hair. Dear, dear. Long, long.

Used items he had moved to one side and stacked symmetrically where possible. Discarded items of clothing worn beyond restoration and aged beyond belief, he folded with appropriate tenderness. After all, had not Mother almost smuggled these originals through Customs?

Items probably meant to remain in his care, he placed in the hip-bag. There, he found squares of soft cloth already provided for the wrapping of the knife, fork, spoon, one beaker, mirror, scissors, comb and brushes . . .

'Now how,' he said to Sam, 'am I to proceed with this hip-bag of conjuring tricks, sword, scabbard, dog on lead, and umbrella as well? The sun is about to set; no rain; no expectation of dew. I'll look like Grandfather Mannerheim missing a screw. What do I do if I meet a dragon? Jettison all except fuel?'

Unused items he left as they were. The honey, the wine, and especially the nuts which proved to be raw. But he incorporated the leftovers into his design, disciplined by a feeling that he was on a curve and was not meant to mess around. All wit, energy, ingenuity and nerve were on immediate call. But not for honey. Sticky stuff. Tricky stuff.

Honey hit this child, Father said, like a shot of Vitamin B12 in the veins of the aged and infirm who might be seen dancing across the skyline before they dropped dead.

Wine made the child sleepy. Thank God, Father said, that there's something to drive this creature to his bed. And raw nuts generated gas and were to be avoided in company; a principle warmly supported by the rest of us, Father once said.

Aloud, Knut growled: 'I believe I hear you, old man. Get lost.'

'Which means,' Knut said, 'there's not much more at this juncture that I'm able to do. A cunning table it was the minions set. But, for future reference – the Universe, I guess, still being packed with carefree cows and chickens – I could've gone for a cheese omelette. I make clear my partiality; cheese omelette is the best and its preparation is not tiresome.'

Knut felt a memory breaking through, without reason: a memory of a nineteenth century hymn.

Good God, no, thought Knut. What next?

It was a hymn not often heard in his former life, Knut not being keen on hymns, especially those long on sentiment. But this, more than a time or two, had struck to the heart. Its recall was linked without reason to the sharper hits scored by that classic buffoon, Cameron Cassidy, a kid at school who once denied him the title of National Champion, Junior Foil. All that hype from his cheer squad of mature friends and family who should have known better. Who should have fought fairer. Why should a buffoon tangle with a discreet little hymn?

> *Day is dying in the west,*
> *Heaven is touching earth with rest;*
> *Wait and worship while the night*
> *Sets her evening lamps alight*
> *Through all the sky.*

No doubt this was followed by the refrain, of which not a word came to mind and a second verse was remembered only fragmentally.

Now why, thought Knut, has *that* come crowding down memory lane to remind me of Cassidy and his lousy family and his stupid tricks?

'Time must be short, Sam. I don't like nice little hymns turning up with weird associations.'

Knut thus beginning to buckle on his belt. He adjusted the hip-bag with personal effects to the right, but was foxed by the scabbard.

What did one do with a scabbard?

Like what would one do with a codpiece?

Knut was hoping it was right when it felt less like a truss and more like a Colt .45.

Then, taking up his sword, he closed his grip on its shocking weight with a shiver. Five hundred grams for a foil. A mere flick of the forefinger. This was like a crowbar.

How deep is my chest? How broad are my shoulders? How strong are my arms? How fast can I run the other way? If I try to use this thing I'll be dead.

I bring to your attention, Sire, three years of daily self-torture at the crossroads in front of the mirror, forging the body. Who wants to look like he's been reared on take-aways? I did not anticipate that life would be advising me it hadn't made a man of me. But it wasn't in the picture that I'd be prancing and dancing with a *crowbar*!

Yet shouldn't I be dead already, back there somewhere along the track? At the foot of the cliff? In the mud at the bottom of the waters? Or offshore with Sam clasped about my neck? Or is survival to be found in one's attitude of mind? Does one wear any kind of sword like a foil and handle it like a breeze; does one swim the miles with a sam about one's neck, no matter what?

Face to face with a warrior demon or a warrior man, how long would I last with a foil? But, maybe with a sword like this . . . !

Hence, with a characteristic rush of the blood to the head, Knut was suddenly on his toes, prancing and dancing, and declaring that it really *was* like lead.

But giving the sword its say. Allowing it to plant him here and carry him there. Giving it a voice in the affair and a view to express. Sam wisely electing to view this spectacle from a distance.

'Sam! Come back!'

Sir, said Sam, my breed treats danger with caution. I advise you accordingly. Would you have me drag your sled from thick ice into thin? I toe the party line until you learn to handle that thing.

'Sam . . . Come back!'

It's a dog's life, Sam said, when little boys grow up. All sams love little boys and girls. Sams gladly sell themselves into servitude. And get stuck. Why wasn't I born a don't-care-cat?

'Sam, I was about to put you on the lead.'

You should have made that clearer, sir. A sam is not a sam until his human runs behind! Well and good. But only for an evening stroll. A short distance one way. A short distance back! You must understand we are where we are because it's the safest place for the night. It's not in anyone's mind, I'm sure, that we should be anywhere else before morning. The table, sir, under the canopy, under the fringe, is a better bed by far than you'll get anywhere ahead.

There are one or two matters, thought Knut, to think through, before we make the move. I must accept that we're under surveillance, though by what method or means or by whom, or upon what manner of screen? Who knows? To date, what might have appeared on this screen?

Yesterday the sun went down on a mountain, steep and barren, long suffered by me. A mountain in a vast world of water. But there, at the end, I met Sam and a person, a person of some kind, who moved me into a disturbed and disturbing dreamtime which may have lasted a night or a year of nights or a thousand years of nights. From which, early this day, in some way, I emerged with Sam. And from which high place, on the lower reaches of this ziggurat, I guess, we plunged into the waters and out of which we emerged in due course. Where I raised myself a step or two, slept a while and awoke on the ceremonial stairway of this ziggurat in broad light of day. Of Sam, there was no sign.

I climbed the stairway as if it were a ladder heading for the sky. There I found myself among the ghosts of a night with Aunt Ingrid. And from there I came on to this table and here I closed my eyes and gave thanks in various ways. When I looked around, Sam had come and I was still on the ziggurat, the same that had sprung up at dawn.

Now the sun has gone down and on top of this ziggurat while daylight fades, we're confronting a garden centuries old. While light holds, what is it that we and others might see?

This table! For sure! With Sam and me in attendance near the outer edge of a forecourt or piazza, of around fifty metres from front to back, heading off into the distance both ways. The paving has been swept clean by rains and winds through a great many years, I'd say. The piazza is edged at head height by a parapet on both sides looking like walls, extending from the ramps that line the stairway from the waters below. There is no obvious end to these parapets, left or right, suggesting a curve.

Ahead, forty or fifty metres away, this garden of once-upon-a-time, this mass of vegetation, this jungle begins. In there, it's already turning dark. Father used to play tricks of this kind. Setting great buildings down in arboretums with themes and motives so mischievous and mean I could hear the hatching of them from outside his door. But away up here? And planted in soil carried bucket by bucket long ago from God knows where? Enough to make the labour of the pyramids look enlightened.

Well, friends and enemies, here we stand, Sam and I. Prepared to defend each other; make no mistake. But if Sam is a question without obvious answer, that's your concern, not mine!

Under my right arm, I carry an umbrella. With pictures, it seems. I shall refer to them on the first rainy day.

The sword, exquisitely significant, is still bearing like a crow-bar against the left leg. A vigorous challenge for me and for all.

Human habitation? No sign? But the rough-hewn table is set to raise the questions. Resident humans, if any, having had time to welcome me with trumpets and the waving of flags. Or with battle-axes and bullets. Yet I remain alone, as always, in human terms. But is it the nature of hostile majorities to fear a lone invader without armour or little Mustangs or battleships in support? And is it not the nature of humans at peace to open their doors?

Which again revives the mystery of an Adam without Eve. It becomes my need to find this lady whilst I'm able to perform. And she needs to be similarly inclined. Neither too young nor too jaded; too ancient nor too faded. I do not invent these conventions: it was the woman who bore me, raised me, and explained it all in unequivocal terms. But I am not fancy-free. I am not uncommitted. And I am not confused.

Friends and enemies, my demeanour on your surveillance screen may suggest that I'm too well primed on principles and perplexities to handle rugged matters of a practical kind. Do not be misled. I stand as confident as the king on the scaffold that my future is ordained.

To myself, I put the question; does the beard make the man? Or does my unexpected pleasure in the measure of body hair suggest that the boy isn't all that far behind?

And you, Sam! By now you should be a dog of obedient mind. When I command you to move ahead, I will not be requiring you to *bound*! No dragging me off my feet as if I were a sled!

Out in front, allowing for any light that remains, the path that
we see entering our wild and woolly garden looks more of a
track for four-legged creatures like Sam. How many four-legged
creatures and of what kind, shuttling back and forth, does it
take to keep flagstones so smooth and swept and clean? Perhaps
I should just get on with it or I'll be arguing for years.

'*Sam!*'

Sam turned a wary head.

'A sudden thought! You were YOUNG on the mountainside.'

We were young together, sir, long before the mountainside.

'At sunset yesterday I'll swear I was seventeen.'

No, sir. By no means. Sunsets and yesterdays are human ideas.

The path . . .

'Sam, it can't be far to wherever it goes, wherever it might be.
This isn't a wilderness; it's the seventh level of a ziggurat; the
accessible top. It's got to be smaller here than lower down. And
it's got edges and a parapet. It's *confined!* So let's get crackin',
Sam. *Mush.*'

We're not in the snow, sir. It's no sled that I'll be pulling.

'Come on, Sam. Let's go!'

Correct terminology, sir, should not be difficult. Words of one
syllable. Ape-like grunts. Given in command.

'Sam. Mush. Mush.'

If you insist, sir, but it'll be rough. You'd do better travelling
light!

Into the garden. Onto the narrow, slightly curving path. Into
the jungle on long, stumbling, stretched, straining strides pro-
ducing from Knut a series of cries.

'For pity's sake, Sam!

'Ease up, Sam. Ease up!

'You're not pullin' a bloody sled!

'STOP, STOP, STOP!'

Certainly, sir, Sam said. In due course, adding: Now try extending your commands to words like SIT and STAND. Like WAIT, STAY, COME, HEEL. Tune in on that idea and hold to it.

'Sam . . . Sam . . . What you do to me.'

All in love, affection and war, sir; all in admiration.

'Come on, Sam. Let's have another try. But quietly. Quietly, Sam. Easy, Sam.'

I stress that you are making a mistake, sir. We should be heading the other way. Out of this, not into it. This is not the place to be in the dark unless we go through at a thousand k's an hour.

'No, Sam. No! No! No! I've told you. I'm not running all the way! Oh my gawd. Oh my gawd. SAM, WILL YOU SIT.'

Sam was shocked into compliance.

'And now bloody STAY.'

Sam was staying, as if stunned.

'You wait on me, Master Sam. You're pushing me. I'm the human. I make the decisions. You can say to them as I'm sure you will, "I was only the dog. I was doing what I was told." But I'm the human and they'll give me the bill.'

Sam heaving with the sigh. This jungle, sir. This jungle-jungle is not the place to be. I'm not a leopard. Not a taipan. I'm only me; a sam. The quicker we're through, the quicker we're there. The risks you run by staying here!

'Sam, I said *stay*. Someone said that *stay* was the word!'

I'm the dog. You're the human. I sit and stay.

. . .

Knut thought: it's clear this path isn't straight. Perhaps Sam distrusts it. Perhaps he knows it of old. Perhaps he's in a hurry to get through. Perhaps the curve increases and becomes an issue? Perhaps it goes round and round?

Perhaps it's a garden greater than the Hanging Gardens of Babylon and left to run wild for hundreds or thousands of years. True, it doesn't smell of gardens. It smells like a jungle. And the feeling is of predators around.

'Sam,' Knut said, 'this place must be giving me the creeps. Might it be better to settle for dragons or demons or deities with whom we may bargain? Predators owe nothing to me, but dragons, demons and deities assuredly do. Without people like me they'd never have got their names.'

A trembling had gathered in Knut simply from reading the signs; as if the winds to stir the leaves and ruffle feathers and drive dreadful creatures underground had never blown through here. Knut was in awe, but hanging on hard to control.

Addressing himself, he said: 'What's done is done. I haven't hit back and I haven't turned or run. And I'll not be looking over my shoulder and I swear on the lives of the people I love, I will not dishonour them!'

Knut was wishing, just the same, to place his body aside, to be free of its aches, to bear what had to be borne without suffering endless pain. Only then, when all was done, could he pick his body up again. But coming from within himself was a brisk command he knew he had never learned: *'Sam! Heel!'*

Knut stepping firmly into the dusk, Sam anxiously, obediently, matching pace and stride. Knut taken profoundly by surprise; at once feeling that the separation he had wished for might even have arrived. His spirit to the left, Sam in the middle, his mundane body to the right.

Urgent signals were sounding in Knut's blood, brain and bone; the daredevil in him striving to widen the gap.

A recollection!

Might history have been repeating itself?

Knut was recollecting Father's stark confession of his wartime aircraft, of his little Mustang with wounds that bled fuel and oil and human blood: *a life crisis, Knut. That's what it was. Mine or theirs. No hero me; but no block of salt. My body to the right and my spirit to the left. My little Mustang in the middle. My cause was moral, but pitiless and swift. No thought for the flesh of the enemy, or for my own. I could have been someone else.*

No hero me either, Knut said to Knut, and no block of salt. Body to the right, Father's words, and spirit to the left. No thought for the flesh. Am I not, also, fast with the blade and swift of foot? But I have a problem, Father. In your little Mustang you knew what it was about. But I have no certainties and cannot say whether my adversary is friend, foe, demon, little god, big god, or the Great One Himself Who Reigns Supreme.

I'm human and alleged to be free. I have been given dominion over my little world and over me. Genesis, Chapter One. But has my adversary, at one and the same time, savaged and succoured me?

The clock stops.

The bomb drops!

No clock and no bomb, but in effect it was the same.

Knut said aloud: 'By God, savaged and succoured at the same

time. Not by one, but by two. By the left hand and the right. By the great good and the great wrong. Opposed.

'One at my left and the Other at my right. And like Sam at heel, I'm caught in the middle and have been there from the start.

'Everything comes in pairs. In opposites. Good and evil. Love and hate. Woman and man.

'This must mean that Eve is here.

'If she isn't, what can life be about?'

OF KINGS AND
CAUSES

*In which shades of the past
attempt to communicate with
Knut in his strange Universe.*

HAIL TO THEE, our star, our son, our one and only dearly beloved.

We are love in darkness, spirits of the flesh that made thee flesh, dear son. We are the ones who made thee from our passion and our love. So when we thunder, do not walk in fear of us. Even our thunder is love.

Incline thine ear. Incline the two. For we have drawn close, reaching out, seeking thee longingly, lovingly, even close enough to touch. But we are here and you are there, each unseen, indivisible, but apart.

Uncounted generations have peopled our world since last we spoke, one evening early on the night of July 3–4, and then were torn apart. Each generation as it has passed, we have counted on our aching genes, searching for your voice through the generations of planet Earth; all generations freely heard by us, but never seen by us, suffering in their pitiless seas of mud, each and all as invisible to us as our own dear son.

Give thought to our darkness, to our hundreds upon hundreds of conceptual days a year apart. All but a thousand years on. All but a thousand times have we returned to seek for thee, to search, to listen, to mourn, though knowing you were not among us with the dead; knowing your body had not died as had ours. We have returned again.

Now here you stand, we are told, most splendid, alive and well, like some lusty lad deeply tanned or some Polynesian king. And, as rumoured, with this ageless dog beside you, on you stride; our joyous confirmation that you truly live. Oh, well done, our star and our sun, to have cracked the egg and crawled within.

Take note, dear one: great loves and great hates alike survive the mortal states. If we have failed to make this clear as well as loud, so be it, even if our hymn of love is not heard by thee, but is only felt.

Our one begotten, bewildered, exalted son. You must know we love thee still. You must know we bleed to be with you in your heart.

Do take care. Do not bruise or break. Do not rest before the work is done, our son; head high, strong arm, straight eye; for already you have slept the ages long.

Heaven and Earth have moved for you; by a league or two. By God, the pull on those strings and cords and ropes and hawsers and gravity rings! The planet has been moved for our son, moved for our son, moved for him, to correct the evils of what Mankind had done.

Do not go so far from us again. Hold to the spirit until you come and we'll have a party, lad, and in the name of justice, justice shall be done.

Be assured, at private times, we'll never be the eye in God's sweet sky, though an ear we may be, as one so dear to us once was. Go find your Eve, dear son; with our blessings; with our prayer; though we know not where she is. For there is no sight of her or sound of her. There is no sign. But this Universe is not for understanding by lesser breeds of men.

Put thy sword aside. It is not the wisdom of one who builds. Do not act from idle pride as if you were nothing but our son. We have our virtue but too often were bent upon the kill; for which there was fair reason that no longer can apply. YOU dare not kill. For most of what you see is all of it there is, until all is built again.

> Dear God, he comes towards his journey's end.
> Why is it we cannot tell him who he is?
> Why must we suffer so for begetting him?
> We weary of gods as once we wearied of men.
>
> Do take care of his dear flesh and blood.
> Who else can? Who else will?
> We have tried, but do not know if we have crossed
> The bridge.

Sire, ours is such a little world, so mauled and spoiled and soiled by greed and foolishness; so far from the palaces where you live.

Hear our cry.

Hear our prayer.

Take care of him, for he is the one.

OF KINGS AND GODS

*Knut considers the conflict of
the left hand and the right.*

Eve? Where might she be?

God, what a foolishness. What an idleness.

What an improper fancy.

What has Knut Canute to do with Eve and the stories of the garden? It was an alluring thought for the son of a national treasure like Richard What's-his-name, but it was also a vanity equal to any conceit of that national treasure in the lusty fullness of his prime.

Knut summing up, but bashfully: 'I think I might have gone for Eve.'

In fairness, was there ever a man of romantic mind who would not kindly have considered the magic of Eden's garden where the Euphrates ran down to the sea? A most appealing thought, thought Knut, which almost shocks the Luther in me. This Eve, what is she but my grandmother a million times removed?

We really must not kid ourselves we're Adam and his dog. Pardon me while I pull my side together and stitch me up again. It's nothing, comrades. A mere appendix. It happens all the time.

But who's that adorable creature I spy with my little eye under the fig tree, emerging from her trauma so charmingly grown? Yet who made *me*, Sire, as I am. Your left hand or Your right? You must claim a modest share of blame. And who put me on this track through the garden with Sam?

I'm not stitched into this theory of lefts and rights. And not, upon reflection, excited by the idea of separating from myself. It leaves open a way for outsiders to rush in. And puts you, Sire, if accounts are correct, in conflict with Yourself at the centre where Good is in charge but Evil goes on working its tricks.

Whilst not wishing to bruise the apple, I state my distrust of extremes by suggesting that good and evil are but two views of one and the same scene. Which points to the presence of an invasive mind that might have challenged my convictions and overruled my right to say what I mean.

This mischief deepens the rift between right and left and right and wrong. The very same feeling I had in the dark outside Father's door as I listened when young. The same yen to run from the ripping within. I remember the shreds I'd found on the floor; some great dream, some great plan torn to tatters by the man.

Father. I have the feeling. I know you're here. I feel you near. Go away. Would you wreck my dreams along with your own? Your torn dreams are too short a step from me. They fence me all around.

Is it nothing that I could have been set apart for a special task? Is it nothing that there might be something *I* must do? Might this explain my pain? A work to be accomplished by the boy who listened, disturbed, outside your door. You threaten, I fear, to tear me up like a less than perfect plan.

All along you've known where I'd be. All along you've known I was alone. Now, in at the kill, do you show your hand?

The free-born, Father, are free to be what they are inclined to be. Fathers are free. So are sons. I say God chooses not to foretell. Each human is a god-that-could-be. Whether one's father is the king and one's mother the queen or just someone in for a quick thrill. God may have the right to try me, Father, but you have none.

Fame is sweet, I believe. But one wins no votes in Heaven for destroying one's kin. For the life of me, Father, did I plan, plot, corrupt, or kill? Did I fail to perform what you asked? I lived my life to please you. But was it some game you were playing as you left that night for *The Turn of the Screw*?

I've done my reading. All the world loves a lover, except the loser. Were you a virgin at seventeen?

Go buy yourself a walking-stick, old man. Go book yourself a pew. I need supporters of simple mind. An army fed on myths that can stand the rigours of time. Round here myths are fouling the drains and stinking the air and the place is lousy with dragons and demons and leopards and trolls and a sword so heavy I can't believe. Last thing I need is a wicked old man crawling up through the drains.

For God's sake, go find yourself a girder. Go draw yourself a plan. Go raise another family.

Death, dear Father, before you muscled in, was stalking this jungle, but we were coping, Sam and me. Scarcely a stride have we missed on this march through, and not even God knows what Death will be coming at next! My mind should be where my sword should be; out in front, clearing a swath through the dusk.

Who can say if you betrayed me? Who knows but you? Go away, Father. Go away. Sweep the fragments from your floor and build a monument to Man. Stick your name on it in lights, but leave me as I am.

Bale out, old man; your Mustang's in flames.

Knut made a grasp for the hilt at his waistband, heat charging from within. Knut made a wish for the swift and elegant draw, for the spinning of the sword like a Colt .45. For the scattering of trolls scuttling for their holes. For the melting of monsters and the confusion of plans in mischievous minds, but stubbing his toe instead!

'Damn!'

Knut striving again to extricate the sword. It would not come. Not enough arms or hands, or too light on expertise. What with sandals and dog leads and umbrellas and legs and sams and branches and twigs and irregular paving stones and a tearing of the spirit and an aching of limbs and a sudden sickness to the soul . . .

What with a striding on in a dead-end light.

What with night dropping like a bird shot from the wing.

'Now,' Knut said, 'before day's begun, we've got bloody night! How long's day supposed to be here? Long enough for a morning swim? Long enough to climb the stairs? Long enough to say your prayers? Long enough to snatch a bite and take a walk to settle it down? Who but me bloody cares?

'Sam, sit!'

If that's your attitude, sir.

Sam sat.

But, sir, I'd rather not. For there's a gulf between the bark of the human and the wisdom of the dog who sorts the sounds and puts names on the smells. This, sir, is an unsafe place.

Knut said: 'I should be overawed. Or terrified. Or numbed. But I'm angry and frustrated and in the bloody dark again, hanging on to a bloody dog.

'I'd feel less naked showing the steel and waving it around. Are swords given to be sheathed? To Hell with the bloody thing. Is it too heavy to move or have I screwed it in? By the time I'd have it dancing and prancing, my head would be on the ground. We've also got our Sam; whose opinion I'd value; there's no one else around.'

Sam said: I remind you that a well-bred worm is superior to a length of steel. As for the bedraggled heap you dragged ashore way back in once-upon-a-time, it's each to his element, sir. On ice or snow the sam challenges the bear, as many a ghost of many a bear will confirm.

'Sam,' Knut said, 'we can't go on without means of defence. This bloody sword; I might as well unbuckle it and put it out with the garbage for recycling into ploughshares. What do we do with it? Drop it where we stand and come back in the morning to deal with dragons, demons and leopards of similar mind? Or charge blindly on, hacking our way to Hell? My vote? My opinion? We've come as far as we're going and we're not going back. We're staying right here. I hope that pleases you.'

Sir, Sam said, it does not, but dog gladly lives and gladly dies on Man's decision. For all dog's imperfections, Mankind is the reason why dog is.

CHAPTER
THIRTY-SIX

BLOODY SAM

The great debate between
dog and man.

'Sam!' Knut whispered it internally, where Knut was of the opinion that only Knut would hear. 'Sam, I'm suggesting a smart move a short distance to the right. I'm now strongly inclined to leave the path, but not to the extent that we can't find our way back. A sideways dash into the sticks executed unobtrusively. No barking, Sam, or I'll wring your bloody neck. By these means we may avoid encounters with passers-by during the night.'

A minor point long in need of making, sir.

'I've no idea,' Knut went on silently, 'why we should be in a jungle prowling about on top of a ziggurat. No doubt teeming with wild life, much of it with claws and prominent jaws and an appetite for raw meat of human origin. Which, I warn you, it will forego for the raw meat of dog at any time.'

Nature, sir, said Sam, has shared a confidence or two with us dogs concerning survival in locations of this kind, which we carry from generation to generation. If you made the same effort to understand me that I make to understand you, there's no saying what you might learn. Sadly, sir, the intelligence of your species is squashed; the brain bearing all that weight when you sit down.

'We,' Knut said, so much above a whisper that he gave himself a start, 'should remain on guard all night. Turn about. No matter how long the night.'

Knut was keenly aware of the value of silence, but admitted the importance of expressing the view: 'I have suspicions about these nights of ours. They've shot my statistics to tatters and left my crossroads in ruin. There appears, Sam, to be no respect for a human point of view built upon observations passed down at awful cost to life through thousands of years. Humans have been hanged, drawn, quartered and burnt alive, Sam, for their virtue and opinions.'

In these latitudes, sir, Sam said, I have noted that nights do not behave as other nights do. But being on guard is another matter. We should serve our watches jointly, your arm about my shoulders to keep you comforted and secure.

'Perhaps,' Knut added, 'it would be better if both of us remained on deck all night through, to give us the confidence that comes from knowing we're not alone, even if one of us is only a dog.'

Sighed Sam: Which is all we can do in the circumstances as arranged by you. But I believe, sir, it'd be better to move on and leave this place behind. I smell creatures I'd rather not meet. They'd scare the living night-lights out of you.

'Let's hope, Sam, the night doesn't last a year.'

A depraved idea, sir, that one might expect of a witch, a warlock or the builder of a ziggurat, perhaps. I hope you came upon it by chance.

'I'm certain, Sam, that we'll be safer off the path in a position we can defend . . . *Sam!* Where have you gone? How could such a brainless nit have slipped his leash? *What shall I do without bloody Sam?*'

Sir, first grow mentally, just a little, but not to a greater height. You're already imposing enough in poor light, though complemented at closer quarters by your immaturity. I stress, there's a time to let rip; to let the world know you're coming through like a runaway truck. In poor light, sir, you'd unnerve them. As for my *symbol of brotherhood*, my so-called leash, it's a significant component of your own mystique! My lead remains in your right hand, crossed over to the left, as it should be. I, too, am where I should be, though not as close as I would prefer to be in the interests of your security. I'd rather be tucked under your arm.

Woof.

A cautious *woof*, sir. To direct your attention larboard! That is, to the left, the side where the well-trained dog is usually to be found. A well-trained human, sir, would be aware of this. That's the idea. Over here, sir. Now *peer* a little.

'For God's sake, mate,' Knut said, 'what are you doing over there? You witless hound. I've stood as much as I can stand.'

The name, sir, said Sam, is 'Silver Czar'. And you're a trial yourself much of the time.

'Oh, to Hell with it,' Knut said. 'Shouldn't we just get on with it and keep going? Fortune favours the brave, you know. Too much fooling around, my dumb friend. Everything's so bloody difficult.'

I've yet to meet a human, Sam said, who doesn't get insultin' when us dogs are around. All these humans suffering until all but out of their minds. Give a thought to the dog's life, sir. To getting thrown out into the wet, the wind and the grey. Nature'll take care of us, you say. My comment being a single heavy sigh. Yet through all these lawless years and the reigns of kings and queens and the rise and fall of in-betweens, faithfully keeping my feet clean and getting born repeatedly to be on hand when your time came around. Very tiresome, sir. Very tedious.

I could've made much of myself by now. I fancied me as a comet, you know, hell-bent, Earth bound, chuckling all the way, rubbing me hands, the biggest bang in a billion years, except for worrying about ducky little sams. If ever there was a darling, it's got to be the baby sam.

And the humans, sir; here and there and everywhere; without us what would they do? Who would they pat on the head to make them feel good? Who'd herd their reindeer? Who'd pull the sled? Who'd welcome them when they blundered upstairs, the worse for too much of a good thing? Who'd have quietly warmed the bed? I'd have made a rotten big bang.

Now I note we're progressing with purposeful strides as at obedience trials. Fine training for humans, sir. Us dogs go along for the ride. Reminding me of my sister, you know. Companion Dog Excellent. Referring to her disciplined response to human command! A kind of super sam. All a bit of a bore for the rest of us.

Well, I guess if we're to get burnt, as we certainly shall, sir, we might as well proceed. Though I've been this way before, sir, as I've been trying to tell you, but you're so thick in the head!

There'll be no chance, sir, to warm your bed. The door's wide open, but there's no way in.

CHAPTER
THIRTY-SEVEN

THE HELMSMAN

Knut begins to realise that
Sam is a fellow creature to
open the doors and shut
them behind.

Knut became visible after a fashion, making a show of striding, as if he passed through here each evening taking the air, but was aware of a recklessness that echoed of a dawn in deep water. Or, perhaps, as if this were Sebastian Street approaching Johann. As if Mother, Father, cats, gnomes, traffic surveys and sound-proofed door signed KMC were about to welcome him home, beard and all.

Sam was the helmsman. A creature proving to be worthy, confident and alert, even if scatterbrained. Knut hoping he was a creature with knowledge of where he was heading. Knut making a statement of dependence that the helmsman wore proudly, out-strutting the show ponies, out-strutting his human.

We're coming, Sam said, to the jungle; to the whisperings and murmurings of predatory creatures in hiding. Take care, you villains, you gluttons, you felons who offend the eye, the nose, the spirit and decency. Beware of my human or you'll not see the morning.

Here we come, Sam said to the demons, especially to those with whom he was familiar. Return to your craters and pits; to your haunts and lairs and books; to your dens and pens and odious pursuits; to your cellars and caves and deeps and depths. Do not foul the sweet air that enwraps my human.

Stand clear, Sam said to the dragons; especially to those known to him. We come in darkness as foretold. Not as thieves to rob you of gold or carry off your children. Do not challenge us. Do not dare. Beware. Do not invoke the power of my human, for only the Devil protects fools.

Knut thought: I wish I could say where the compass points lie. I haven't given thought to them in quite a while. I used to regard them as the rhyme and reason for being at A, B, or C. Not to know where they are is to lose one's credentials. They're the fundamentals by which one functions. Ask any toadstool.

The Southern Cross was institutional; it was the tree and I was a bough. Blindfold me in the dark. Turn me round. And round again. Finding my Cross was a breeze. The absence of the stars I lived among affects my belief in me.

There are black holes inside of me and one memory only that's as fresh as yesterday ought to be: that ledge with bones, an eagle, a leopard, and the young dog who came.

It's not surprising there's a panic or two.

From that ledge I climbed the mountain with Sam and with a human of some kind, greatly aged, of awesome strength, sufficient to open the door of the mountain and take me inside. She loved me, softly, caressed my hair and sang me to sleep in words I didn't understand. Wonderful words. Magic. Was it really my Grandmother Mannerheim? It was a strange,

strange sleep of indeterminate time, during which I grew to be a man.

I came out of the mountain and plunged into the waters. I came out of the waters onto a ziggurat. I climbed a stairway into the sky. I broke the fast of the day, the year, or the age. From which I walked on with Sam into a jungle which may not be as foreign as it seems.

In whole or in part, what do I remember of this switch from the boy into what I have become?

It was not a measured change to observe, encourage or correct. Flesh, muscle, hair, bone, all present in appropriate measure, it seems. Properties surely not to be acquired in the deep freeze or by lying dormant like the forest seed until awakened by a fire.

I have the *look* of a grown man, but where are all the years of growing with my girl Nanette? Did she walk, symbolically, down to the sea, to wait for my ship to come back in? Or did she dance into the sunset, uncaring, with all the guys running behind?

I put it to you gods out there. Am I supposed to be intrigued or awed? The truth is I feel mad enough to drive a fist through the first brick wall I see.

Knut was striding it out; an eye to the unfolding night sky; a low-key expectation of a rising moon.

'Not two moons, please,' Knut said. 'Not an hour ahead or behind. And not a dozen. Not a sky full of moons squabbling for a share. Just one like the one I used to have; the lovely moon I had before.'

At another time, Knut said: I wish to be where I want to be. Any part of *home* will do! Any latitude, any longitude, as long as I can get to the corner of Sebastian and Johann by any means at all . . .

Later: keen eyes to the sides and ahead, hearing tuned for sound and an awareness, a sensitivity, for what could be coming behind. Creations of the mind. Creatures in line astern like those met by Alice in her Wonderland, or by Dante in his Inferno. By Jurgen journeying through love land. (Top shelf. Third left. Father's library. Faded Penguin binding, 1940.) But there was nothing concretely seen except masses of darkness and a continuing curve between the solids at his feet and the scimitar of sky. Knut praying his helmsman heard more, saw more and smelt all.

The sky's an issue, but it's air that I'm breathing. Might the air of Earth happen twice? Or might my ziggurat have survived from days as distant as Sumer and Akkad and Babylon and Ur?

Father, might the waters around us be the ancient Euphrates heading for the sea? Or the deluge of Noah's time? Or the melting of the icecaps as foretold? Questions of place and history of this kind disturb me.

Thank you, God, for Sam. I believe he knows where we're bound. It's as if I were blind and had found a fellow creature to open the doors and shut them behind. Yet he is one with whom I cannot discuss or exchange a single word. Is it the nature of life when life's in balance, for Nature to take care of us? Is it the nature of Dog to arrange it and bring it into line?

'I've been rude to you, Sam.'

Points run about square, sir.

. . .

Sam making contact with Knut's left knee.

This is the place, sir. It's time.

Knut checking Sam on the lead.

'We're there,' Knut said. 'We have come to where I've been heading all the time. I feel it in my bones.'

IT'S TIME

Yet no one's here but me and a
dog of little wit: about Time
and Knut's beard.

The dreamings of other years. Knut called them up from the distances of his mind.

A million years of Earth time, he thought, may not be critical in some departments of science, but they declare the reality of the marvel of a million orbits by our brilliant planet about our precious, if slightly worn star. This brilliant planet, this curiosity, this Earth, travelling in company with straggling agglomerations of lethal radiations, venomous vapours and great lumps of mindless rock hurtling out of nowhere intent upon mayhem. Launched by delinquent gods letting off stink bombs in the science room and throwing stones on the way home.

Mathematically, these million Earth years of ours shouldn't pose a problem for persons past grade three, but in terms of human time they exceed our understanding and lie outside the grasp of very clever humans indeed . . .

Knut consulting further with himself: Consider a hundred revolutions of this brilliant curiosity about this fiery flaming furnace, Old Man Sun, in whose direction we may not turn our adoration for longer than the blink of an eye except at peril of losing the eye. A mere hundred journeys; a frivolity; a formality; but rarely experienced by anyone we know.

Knut was giving comprehensive consideration to these issues in an instant or two, as was his custom. Continuing: Where do I stand in regard to these ridiculous concerns of the human mind? This night I have travelled kilometres along a continuing curve. A spiral. A distance for measuring, toe to heel and heel to toe, in thousands of feet. Declared on the authority of a million years of human feet stepping through forests and jungles, across deserts and grasslands, rafting down rivers, drifting across seas until they came to where they had to be.

How far am I along the trail? Am I to measure it in leagues, miles, yards and feet or decimals?

I recall the tempests raging through the darkest recesses of the house at the corner of Sebastian and Johann Streets: 'Bloody kilometres! An outrage upon the prince of languages. A legislated compulsion to translate noble distances into witless decimals. As mindless as swallowing your teeth.

'To this day my heart remains afire,

My spirit he leaps:

I have wings on my feets:

For the love of my lady

I still could run a mile.

'Dear, dear,' Knut said then, relieving his person of items he had carried from the table and folding his arms to strike a pose, while Sam said, This unit of measurement, sir. If it's stopping you from doing what must be done, get rid of it.

Thought Knut: I suppose I could do that. No one's here but me and a dog of little wit. What a brilliant idea.

Aloud, he said: 'Why should I not declare, forthwith, that the decimal is an abomination? Let's not think of fingers and toes and tens and twenties. That's all right when one is aged two! All measures forthwith shall be based upon the human foot as the unit, for where would we be without it? Up the creek without a paddle. And all currency shall be founded upon twelve large and lustrous copper pennies, twelve to the shilling which rings in the head as a solid silver shilling should.

Is that so? Sam said. I've managed to my satisfaction on nothing more than a friendly disposition.

Knut was bored with the subject, anyway, and was becoming distrustful of that absence of detail known as total darkness. Ten-tenths cloud had arrived from somewhere, a barrier that protected him from nothing other than the contemplation of the stars. Above, below and on every side, he lay wide open to everything in hiding. Leopards. Lions. Anacondas. Taipans. Mean-minded humans and assorted mythological figures of potent ill will.

'Yet,' said Knut, 'it's always time for rhyme and reason. For example: could I have come this far without a destination on the ticket? Of course not. And seriously, how old do I feel? Have I ever felt different?

Father used to say: 'Great Grandmother Canute, on the day following her ninety-fifth birthday, one hand on hip, complained that age was becoming a burden. She'd been partying until 2 a.m. and lived but five more years, poor darling, less a couple of days. Struck down by a cake of soap, underfoot, at 6.30 in the morning while taking her shower. Cheated by mere hours of her telegram from the Queen.'

How old, Knut said to himself, did *I* look in that small steel mirror? Of a size for Father to have worn in his little Mustang; *Iliad* in right breast pocket, mirror in the left, guarding his heart.

If these thoughts are coming from you, Father, isn't it time you left me to get on with my own? How old, precisely, *did* I look in that mirror? In *my* mirror? The long vaunted dent that deflected the bullet not being in evidence! Without which, as often I have been told, I would not have been born.

So Knut traced the shape of his mirror against his own hard chest, to emphasise the point, but at once suffered a severe contraction of the gut.

Okay, Father. You win. It's your mirror.

Later, Knut said: 'I've read you wrong. You're with me, Father. You're not against me.'

Thereupon, Knut wept.

Well, stick a beard on Peter Pan and what have you got? Grow one yourself when you're looking the other way. You can't rip it off.

No way have I been hanging around waiting for a beard to grow. No way hoping for bloody great strands of wire to sprout from my ears. Am I a deep-space probe? Who wants to look like something that Sam dragged in? I must look all of twenty-five.

Check the red hairs for grey! Maybe I was born looking tired. I must be the oldest virgin unhung.

Where would I have lived this so-called life of mine, whiskers sprouting from the sides while the ages rolled by? Frozen solid. On exhibition? All the little kids rushing home, 'Mummy. Wow. What we saw in the museum today.'

Or had everyone gone to sleep for an age? The planet in deep-freeze mode. The Instant Ice Age. Father halfway through a stride halfway along a girder balancing on one toe. Mother frozen to her keyboard, forefinger on m, halfway through Cootamundra, achieving her mmmmmmmmmmmasterpiece! Several trillion mmmmmmmmmmmmmmmmmmmmmmms.

My opinion, said Knut, is that I spent the Instant Ice Age right here, sleeping off a riotously ill-spent youth. And of late, I've been sleepwalking in circles. When the sun comes up I'll be in sight of Sebastian and Johann. I'll be home. Seventeen when I started, but God knows how old in the morning? Don't let's put it to Old Man Time. Like Father, he'll dodge the issue. They're bound to be one and the same.

Ask Father the time of day and what do you get? A run-down on the joys of witchcraft during the Dark Ages. Or if it's Saturday or Sunday, you get the incompatibility of sport with sportsmanship as it was when he was young. Each a discourse of forty minutes ending with the question, 'Did someone ask the time?'

Early in life it became clear that the nature of Time was linked to the wastage of it. All questions appeared to confuse it. Everything and everyone functioned to private agendas. Even cats, dogs and kids.

'Nevertheless,' Knut said, addressing all creatures secreted around, 'that moon jostling with the clouds begins to look familiar!' Knut was hesitating to break into effusive expressions of thanks, keenly aware of the awesome alternatives if it proved not to be so. But then he was able to add, 'Well, Sam, my friend; it is our old mate; the man in the moon.'

Knut carefully sitting in the midst of the items he had brought from the table and carried through the great garden or jungle. 'Enough's enough,' he said. 'Let's wait for the morning. We need Old Man Sun to show us around.'

Rain began to fall. Heavily.

'Bloody where did I put that umbrella?'

Then Knut raised it and said: 'Come on under, Sam. Room for two.'

THE FOCUS

*Knut is berated for not
respecting what time has
done for him, for humanity –
for not respecting body and
planet and dog, for not
recognising justice. Then he
comes upon a lion . . .*

Knut awoke, huddled and wet. There was no rain. Left hand to the shaft of the umbrella tucked into his thighs; building an abstract picture of his surrounds disciplined by an uncommon presence of mind.

Some deity or devil or demon or dragon in playful mood could have been sending an urgent signal:

Lie doggo, kiddo.

Message received, thought Knut. And entered in log. But what's this *kiddo* stuff? Kindly note I've stopped being a kid.

Knut then dismissing the urge to stretch a leg and ease an arm. Betraying nothing except the visible; breathing heavily as if sleeping; hoarding oxygen. Fine-tuning his hearing; ranging for thought waves of interest. Sending out feelers on numerous wavelengths like threads of smoke.

Damn' silly thing to do, thought Knut; dropping off in the

middle of rain. But it's daylight now, early and warm; steamy; and me smelling like ashes of violets, evaporating.

I hear birds, I reckon; but where? Maybe I wouldn't want to know. They could be harpies. I hope this umbrella works back-to-front. Put it up to generate rain. Put it down to get a blow-dry. Leading to the complementary question: bloody Sam? Where? Gone until pangs of loyalty tell him he's hungry. Well, he's got his own agenda along with the rest of us, that most human of dogs. Not on hand when needed. Having done the big flit before; now again; dragging his lead behind for getting strung up in trees and caught by leopards and lions. Lead still in my hand! No dog at the end. Cunning bloody Sam. Watch it, my friend; mere dog mixing it with man!

Time, boy, to keep your head.

That old devil or deity is coming through again!

Knut bristling: 'I value my head as much as you value yours.'

Time, boy, to be mature.

'I haven't twitched a muscle. I hardly recognise myself. Doing everything right but still gettin' picked on by the elderly and infirm.'

Time, boy, to give Time a chance to overtake. You've been unconscionably hard on Time and not to your credit.

'Tell me what Time's done for me?'

We issue no ultimatums or explanations and do not speak of extra-dimensional concerns. We speak only of the flesh, the ulti-mate non-renewable concern which we regard as the supreme concern of our little Universe. Humans regard it with such cav-alier disrespect that all other conscious creatures and objects are at a loss. Spirit is spirit; given and sometimes holy; but renew-able in a moment. Flesh and blood and bone refined through the ages in human form is a triumph. To lose the humans here is to lose four billion years.

We have been informed this physical Universe was refined to house the humans who would maintain it and entertain it, even challenge it. That extraordinary opportunity has been dissolved by those for whom it was made. Surely it is apparent that you were set aside to be revived? Choice was neither limited nor unlimited. But we declare that the physical substances of the young Canute, having shown such little regard for Time, are beginning to run out of time.

'I,' said Knut, 'see no logic in that. What have I done to be landed with it? Have I run from anything? Am I running now? Am I failing to do as told? I'm lying doggo like a dead doggo. Am I not giving you my ear? And am I not beginning to wonder whether you answer to the name of Canute or Mannerheim? You don't inspire me or scare me. Out of your own mouths you're second level. I see no justice in your condemnations. I see pique!'

Son of Canute, justice must be seen in relation to where one stands. You cannot complain. You were never out of care. And where, during your recent sleep, has your right hand fallen? There lies the sword. Ready to draw. A mighty weapon for a mighty man. How strong would this man need to be? Stronger than you? Faster on his feet? How practised? How skilled? Or how rusty through the neglects of Time? Be assured, Time has not abandoned you. Yet this Canute, at this moment, would have no need of a dog on a lead to obstruct him. The lead lies lightly across the left hand as you have observed. The right hand is free to draw the sword, which will now come easily, for this is why it was prepared for you.

Then this deity, this devil, this demon or dragon, added: Are you good and ready, my son, to slip the left hand from out and under?

'Of course I'm not bloody ready.'

Why not? You've known an encounter with the Cause would come. Can you leave your life to a dog, even if he be a dog for kings? He cannot be expected to abandon his own agenda entirely. Have you abandoned yours?

'What agenda's that? I'm a football.'

The football has an agenda. To survive for the next game.

'How would I know that? How would you? Are we all footballs?'

You said you were.

'I don't remember.'

It's in the ether. It's said. It's eternal.

'That's bloody unfair.'

So you'd rather be unborn?

'I didn't say that! But I expect of Sam a little loyalty. I abandoned my agenda for him. Who was it that I dragged from that ruinous sea? But I've heard the stories. Who hasn't? The sam who loves all humans, irrespective, and shows the burglar the key.'

We, said the deity, devil, demon or dragon, have given you time to grow to be the man. Through trial we have assisted you to acquire the guile of the ancients. And to the moment, at least, have not removed from you your right to be wrong. We have left you with the beating heart of the boy, against aspects of better judgement.

We have not intruded upon your growth. You are what you would have been. Flex a muscle. Do as we suggest. Check biceps and triceps. Check deltoid. Anatomy; a subject for foils. Check flexor carpi radialis. Check pectoralis major. Check gluteus medius. And sartorius. Are you not sensing the exceptional?

The boy does not need to be told of his prowess. He knows he can run, can leap, can be the leopard, the eagle and the lion? The boy knows that in an instant he can be any creature he wishes to be for as long as he believes.

Not so swiftly moves the man who wields the sword unless he has the soul to flight it like the boy with the dancing feet who flights the foil. Like the leopard and the lion.

Of the million ways through the maze, there is only one. Prove it.

Knut thought, upon opening his eyes: The square I see through the trees, brings to mind Tiananmen. As if in disrepair. Earth bared here and there. Sheets of rainwater slow to drain. Paved in the manner of the piazza way back there, behind, at the top of the stairs.

This square opens from the track that we followed through the wilderness. Which makes it the zenith of the ziggurat. The heart of it. The focus, as it were. I've been marching round it in circles half the night long. A larrikin touch of design that does *not* enchant me.

Which means the building out there at centre is the house pre-pared for the gods, as in 3000 BC. *Our best shall be made ready for Him who comes to lead us into the new way.* Okay. Okay. A beautiful world of magic and wonder always longing for and looking for something better.

Question: why should the house of the gods look like a block-house, as if cannon were about to extrude from the walls?

Troops within, dreaming of their ladies, asleep on straw palliasses on stone floors. Officer of the Watch shrilling through corridors: 'Gun crews at the double.'

Knut versus Gibraltar!

Alternatively, the designer scratching away at his slab of stone, might have been of the opinion it wouldn't hurt the gods to rough it like the rest of us. I've been lying in full view, but if they shot at me they missed.

I've seen this building before.

The only ziggurat I ever saw was Father's in the middle of town and that has nothing to do with this one. And the only lion I've ever met face to face *is three steps away from me, no more.*

SON OF CANUTE

*In which Knut fights
the lion . . .*

'I see you, Lion . . . '

Knut already balanced and balancing.

'Go away, Lion, while you have the chance.'

Knut wondering at the speed of his own moves, not acquainted with the man that he had become. As long before he had sometimes feared for the actions of the boy.

'You're a real lion.'

This is my life, thought Knut. Treat it with care, man. Knut lives here. Remember who you are. Don't fool yourself, man, that you can handle a lion.

The sword drawn, screeching from the sheath. For Knut, it was an exquisite and terrifying sound, the sword at once becoming a rigid extension of his long, strong, steady arm, and a piercing extension of his eyes. The umbrella becoming his shield.

What's this reflection of me that I see in the lion? Seen by Mother in days of indeterminate time.

'Lion. One move and you're down the tube! I run my steel between your eyes and out through the back of you!'

I must, thought Knut, be mad.

'Lion. *Drop!*

'Lion. *Stay!*'

And I do, thought Knut, mean what I say.

The eyes of the lion and the eyes of Knut. A silvered blade and a leap between.

'Lion. I listen to the world and it tells me the world I knew has gone. But here I am and there are you. Does that suggest we share a point of view?

'Give thought, Lion, to Time and its tricks. But swiftly. Samson with the ass's jawbone slew the like of you. But Knut with the sword might make peace with Lion. Samson might not have given thought to the idea.

'Why the awesome aspect, my friend? No need to prove yourself. I'm already impressed. The gods care for you and care for me or we wouldn't have met. But if I lie dead another like me will come. More, I'm sure, lie deeply sleeping on cliff sides, in tunnels and caves, tended by loving spirits greatly aged. But the queue stops here! I'm not edible, my friend. If you make a move I shall be very savage indeed.

'For a moment give thought to Anatomy as studied by you, I'm sure, for Practical Dismemberment. Think particularly of sternocleidomastoid. Mine! Fatal, if swallowed by you for breakfast or tea. You'll choke on it.'

The lion sprang and was in the air and on his way.

Damn, thought Knut, and instantly was farther over, arm tensed and stressed, sword like a needle directed from his quivering right hand, his umbrella the shield.

Knut said: 'Lion! Do drop and stay! What a waste of goodwill. How could any lion be so dumb?'

The lion was in the air and again Knut was elsewhere. 'Lion,' he bellowed, 'sit while I catch my breath. You have a hearing problem? You reckon you're brighter than Sam? Sam's the king and sits when told.'

The lion was in the air and on the way. And Sam, looking splendid and thoughtful, was sitting as told.

Knut, son of Flight Lieutenant Richard Canute, eyes shutting from despair and dismay, flighting his sword across the lion's path. Predicting the point of interception. Spearing the lion through the leading front paw. Pinning him, screaming, as if to a wooden floor, short of Sam by one human stride.

Knut, hand to heart, yelling to the sky: '*Sit still, you stupid lion*!'

And to Sam: 'Stupid dog. Stupid, stupid dog. At bloody heel. At bloody once!'

Sam came and bloody was.

'Are you so dead set on becoming the late Whatever-Your-Name-Is?'

Sobaka Silver Czar, sir, as already detailed at length. But not late. Precisely on time. Setting the example as required. An obligation among dogs to obey orders loud and clear. Who orders dogs but kings? Likewise an obligation among kings. Who orders kings but dogs?

Knut was raising his right forefinger, extending it to above maximum possible length.

'A virtue of dogs, one of the few, they're not able to express an ill-informed view! Speaking generally, lions don't communicate in English either. The Brits might be mad enough to believe it, but I suggest lions communicate in Egyptian or Sudanese.'

Then Knut added: 'I can't stand screaming lions! Will you behave like a king and not an alley rat! You're not severed by a lawn mower or the blunt edge of an axe. It's a clean perforation from the point of a shining silver sword. If you behave, I'll take it out and inspect the damage and at the earliest opportunity boil you an egg. If you don't stop screaming, I'll rip it out sideways and run it between your eyes!'

Fair go, said Sam.

'You pipe down! This is one king who is not going to be ruled by mere lions or dogs.'

Knut was about to fold his umbrella, his shield, intending to tuck it under an arm with a flourish. But then he sighted its more permanent features, the images on its inner surface: among them lions and a swordsman, stylised.

Knut losing several breaths and not folding the umbrella. Taking the point. Continuing to use it as his shield. Advancing upon the lion, raising his right forefinger and peering from behind:

'Step One, Lion. Shut up!

'Step Two. Not a twitch!'

One pace short, arresting it, shield presented a little from the left.

'This is deadly serious stuff, Lion. Take it easy and wear the crown or down the tubes you go. I'll run it through, I swear!'

Thoughts were coming to Knut from afar. Images of boyhood crises. Image One: the taming of Bully Boy Toogood, aged eleven; Knut aged nine-and-a-half. A slugging match in the schoolyard stopped by Tina, Toogood's sister, Grade Three, rushing in: 'Don't you hit my Tom!'

Image Two: Twogood, aged fifteen, perishing of a vicious inherited disease. Knut away from school, rigid in St. Sebastian's, gripping Mother's arm, having words with God:

'You didn't tell me! I didn't know! Don't ever do it to me again!'

Knut was aware of Sam at his left, where the last order had directed him to be. 'What are you doing there, stupid dog? He could kill us with one swipe of one arm.'

Me no speaka da English, Sam said. Me Siberian and just passing through.

'You *dog,* you.'

Knut eye to eye with the lion. 'Beware, Lion. Take care, Lion.'

Still the one step between.

When we get round to these boiled eggs, Sam said, make mine two.

There is, thought Knut, an absurdity here that escapes me.

Unhurriedly, taking the last step, Knut grasped the sword and wrenched it clear in a long second, up from the earth beneath and out through the paw of the lion. Hearing the scream and at once seeing Lion in several adjoining places.

Knut on guard, prancing, dancing, darting between the places.

The lion, bloody and raging.

Gone from Knut's mind was all thought of Sam and further philosophic encounters. Reviewing his life in an instant. Beginning, middle and untimely end. A saga of misfortunes and marvels concluding with a roar of lion-like magnitude issuing from himself: 'Lion, you're stupid.'

Lion, marginally unreal, weaving beyond the tip of the sword at a distance.

'Lion. No!'

Knut not in command, aware of Lion in the air like lightning striking from clouds, but finding himself by extraordinary effort to be elsewhere. Every time at every threat, elsewhere. Labouring against shortages of breath and raging heartbeats. Then observing Lion in slow motion, watching him drop and stay and faint away.

'Good God,' Knut said. Then thought a while. 'Did I try to kill you? Ever? Never. I was keeping myself alive! Pull yourself together.'

Lion made no move and Knut dropped beside him.

'Handsome Lion; beautiful Lion; I couldn't allow it to be me. But should lions faint at the sight of blood?'

I'm back again, said Sam, in the manner of the dog.

'Do you,' asked Knut, 'faint at the sight of blood?'

When it's my own, sir.

'Where the Hell have you been?'

Around, sir.

'Where was the faithful hound and his diversionary moves? Lucky you're dealing with me. You could've been left with Lion.'

That's so, sir. I suppose. But tactics change with situations. When I displeased you before, you called me names for doing my job. I wasn't bred to be abused. I'm a sam. But Lion, I see, gets a pat on the head for staining the land with blood. Well, that may be the proper thing for him. The land where we stand has many times been stained with blood.

Sir, this is holy ground. God is present. Which also means the Devil probably is. It's unlikely you've speared the foot of God, but as much as blood displeases me (I was raised on vegetation, sir, due to extraordinary circumstances), I'll clean his wound and he may limp away if you give him the opportunity. But I do wonder if you have speared the foot of the Devil? Interesting. Or

241

is Lion a creature like Man, born to foolishness and pain? Devil one day and god the next?

If he comes again, I swear I'll sink my teeth through his jugular and bear the cost. God gave you the sword that you might choose. He gave me teeth the same.

WHO SLAYS THE DRAGON?

*Knut explores the ziggurat
further, questions his Universe
one more time, and is on the
way to coming of age.*

The fortress at the centre of the square . . .

Knut was making his way with dignity; sedately; a restrained military step; thinking: this may indeed be a fortress. Defendable against bull-headed cavalry, foot soldiers and swordsmen. But it still could be, as first thought, the ancient lodge made ready for the gods.

It's the zenith and the focus. No designer of right mind would turn the focus into anything less than the focus. Certainly no one like Father.

Which was the stunning thought that provoked the disciplined and internal break in Knut's stride.

Halfway through the stride a punch inside took his breath away, but he stuck with it, kept going, head held high.

No weaving; but making greater demands on air. Managing to stay on course as if unstoppable. Maintaining the image of proprietary rights which could, by God, be critical. Remembering to hold enough back to make the great effort if required. Ever on the ball of the foot; an instant only from the cutting sword, the dancing toes and the war whoop.

Ridiculous, thought Knut. I'm not tried in serious combat, except with something looking like a lion that fainted at the sight of blood.

But now we know where we are and what we've got, and everywhere I've been recognising that man's touch! It's the pieces on the floor of Father's den; the pieces of paper that I picked up and put together again. What can it be but Father's ziggurat?

The ultimate fundamental mass. Gardens on Level Seven and representations of the animal kingdom on Level Six. The definitive non-zoological zoo. Father's time capsule. His monument to Mankind. Leaving only trees and birds and indigenous animals to survive on view. On lower levels, sealed and concealed, were the libraries, the galleries, the museums, the machines and their products; the achievements of the human creature over something like ten thousand years.

'Sam. A quick lick behind. We can't trust Lion. Keep the eye peeled.'

Sam was at heel, but not on the lead. Freedom for Sam to move considered by Knut to be of greater importance than Sam's control. Notably if Knut should become confused.

A distance of two hundred paces more to go: Knut counting and calculating on the darker side of the brain. Translating them into two hundred yards; then into less than two minutes; then into an imminent confrontation with the blank wall, unless it really were a fortress and they mowed him down on the way.

This was one more replay, it seemed, of the recurring theme of the march of the king to the scaffold.

I could, Knut thought, do with three sides to the brain! Perhaps that makes the Napoleons of the world. One side for here; another for there; and one to spare.

In about a minute and a half, will my world crash into reverse? Will everything fly off? In a minute twenty-five? In a minute twenty?

At zero, who knows? Someone must.

Echoes of Father. Images of his little Mustang flying out a hundred and fifty-seven times? Off along one rough strip or another, lurch by lurch; each time fearing his little Mustang might become a bomb and blow up.

Seeing it through a hundred and fifty-seven times for his family, his country, his king and himself. That his duty should be seen and felt by the enemy to have been done. That was Father's program, Knut thought. Now it's mine.

This mystery of Father's mirror, removed from its own century and lodged in uncertain times: Knut was giving thought to the dent made long ago by a fragment of some kind. A mirror greatly smaller than Father's heart. In like manner, greatly smaller than Knut's heart.

There were no external windows ahead. Was it a long, long wall of see-through brick? With the enemy knowing where I am to the inch. If they're human they need to know. If they're not human, they know anyway.

So what spirited me through the ages?

Who gave Sam to me?

Who cared for me, in this ziggurat, underground?

Who placed the symbol of the fire-lighter on the table, along with the sword?

Who re-clothed me?

There's not a gun slot or crevice visible in this wall. No legionnaires or knights with banners or steeds. But I see no way that this can end with handshakes or cheers.

At a hundred and eighty paces, Knut said to Sam, 'Sit. Let's think this through.'

Then to the gods with a sigh: 'You're playing the cards too close. I'm a simple guy.'

To his mother, he said: 'Mother, I've been abusing our man. I feel guilty. I feel troubled. He knew long before I was born what this would be like. He knew it a hundred and fifty-seven times.'

To Father, Knut said: 'It was I, sir, not Mother, who rescued the plans and pinned each fragment back on the drawing board. You never said a word. You left me to assume you had swept it aside a second time and thrown it out with the garbage. Okay. That was your way.

'Sir, the world believed in you. Your plan must have become the scripture. The world found itself a mountain as you specified and fitted it to the plan and made of it the ziggurat, Man's monument to Man. They even left the quarry face faithfully unscaleable at the rear. It was to that face, sir, that I came at first. And it was to the front, sir, that I came at last. Your Jacob's Ladder, brazen and brave, heading for the sky.

'The builders, sir; forgive them for mishaps here and there. They were in great haste. Was it because of imminence of impact with some object coming from Space? Or a rapid poisoning of atmosphere? Or a melting of icecaps and an overwhelming rushing and rising of waters?

'As for me, sir, I have no memory of death, and must assume I did not die. Here, I appear to be alone in the flesh. Scarcely as it should be to handle such a mess. Or are we forever clearing up what others have left?

'Whose mess did Adam and Eve inherit?

'Perhaps it's not a thousand years, sir, that I slept.

'Perhaps it was many thousand.

'But I must find my Eve or even what has survived will be lost.'

Standing at a distance of sixty feet from the confronting wall, Knut was laying aside all extras except the umbrella and the sword. Drawing the sword; tucking the umbrella under his left arm; presenting the sword vertically; and declaring in a loud voice:

'I am Knut Mannerheim Canute!

'I am the only issue of Richard Canute and Madeleine Mannerheim. Not long since, I swore to storm this place. But I will never disfigure what Canute made. Let me see you as you are. Show a face!'

Knut continued to present his sword and received no response.

Sir, Sam said, it's not a great distance to another side for a better view.

'What are they doing to me, Sam?'

You're doing it to yourself, sir.

'You're gnawing my leg, Sam! It might be time to eat, but I have other things on my mind. The pity is, the face of this place has changed. Father had the focus in another form. Sculptured. A sphere. This is strange.'

Knut was firmly closing his eyes and fiercely opening them to glare at a disinterested sky.

Knut versus the Universe. One more try.

...

Mother, Knut said to himself, once told me that life left her without options. Causing her to regard herself as a frustrated tea-bag anxious to be nothing other than a first-class cup of tea. A modest ambition for a woman of modest achievement. But the kettle never boiled, she said. Made a bubble or two and blew the fuse.

I, Knut said to himself, regard myself more as the apple. The unassuming, uncomplicated, high-principled, self-sacrificing apple. Contending with wind, hail, cockatoos, codling moth, canker, rot, fungus and scab, as well as the kids coming over the fence from next door. Being an apple is being in life down to the core, even to the ultimate fulfilment of the king's table.

With a growing sense of the absurd, Knut lost patience with the role of the tin soldier.

'Sam! I give it away! At heel!'

With pleasure, sir. Us dogs like to see our humans play the game with glitter.

Knut checking his goods and marching to the left.

'Watch that lion!'

Watching him, sir, but when we turn the corner, away down there, he'll be out of sight. Lions don't stick to the rules. We would have a better view if we went right.

Knut swinging about and marching right, Sam an instant behind.

That's the spirit, sir, though I'd appreciate the traditional warning of the slap to the thigh. But when briefing you, I forgot.

Whereupon, the lion made his presence heard.

There's your lion, sir.

248

'Sam! Sit! And don't move!'

Not my nature, sir. Got to be where the action is. Why are you leaving me back here on my own?

'Sam! Stay!'

No way, sir; no way.

'Stay!'

The nature of Sam, sir, is to lead his man. To remind his man of my stimulating presence and awesome aspect. Sams never come free and can't bear being left behind!

'Heel, then, as you must!'

Have no fear, sir; Sam is here. Keep the trigger finger nimble and the powder dry.

Knut presenting the fearsome tip of his blade at arm's length, shouting towards Lion: 'One strike will do for you. That's all I'll need!'

Lion, favouring his injured paw, was continuing to lope in.

Knut aiming between the ears and eyes; out through the roof of the mouth into the brain.

'Lion, I wouldn't keep coming if I were you . . . '

At ten paces, Lion was sweeping both forward and back. Dropping and staying. Eyes of man and lion, locked.

Knut murmuring: 'Sam, you'll obey me. You'll *drop*!'

Sam bowing gracefully, in the manner of Lion, curiously creating a moment of privacy. Knut retracting his arm, slowly, and raising his sword to the vertical.

At the crossroads again; Knut's eternal Sebastian and Johann. Eye to eye and nothing between. Lion and man and dog. Nothing except a sword so heavy, so heavy, so heavy that Knut yearned only to put it down.

Here I am, beyond doubt. Looking like someone I never

knew. But with the memories of me. Last known to be alive, distressed of mind, one early morning of July 4, at 1.17. House Captain of Luther at Wittenberg. Devoted son of Richard and Madeleine. Brother of Cynthia, never born. Loving nephew of Aunts Sophie and Ingrid. Cousin of Jacqueline and Claus. Nanette's young man. Her adoring slave. Never more sure of her than she was of me. Our love a memento for having been young together at the same time.

Now, unless I wrongly read the script, I'm the last man alive. The last of his kind. The last man, and without an Eve. I've thought my way down this track many times. It had to happen to someone. Sometime. It has happened to me.

Man belongs on Earth where it's real. Everywhere else is a projection, a reflection of knowledge in vogue at the time. As perishable as words on paper, as images on film, as humans long dead.

I stand, sword in hand, dog to the left, lion in a fog at ten paces ahead, ziggurat beneath, mystery all around, with nowhere to go but on. We three are the Universe. Without us there is none.

The weight of the sword had increased to become unbearable. Knut sheathing it, driving it home, crying within: What am I doing? What have I done? Shut a door. Declared a symbol. Raised a flag.

Knut then unbuckling the belt and placing the sheathed sword at his feet. Where, in a moment, he found himself also to be, on his knees, inviting his Universe to dissolve in bloody slaughter, not for an instant taking his eyes from the eyes of the lion, ten paces removed, fog everywhere else around, all around and in between.

Knut was shaking with his weeping.

Mother said: My honey-bunny slays the dragon of Eden with love and turns him into a pussy-cat.

Father said: That's my son. I salute the king.

CHAPTER
FORTY-TWO

PROTOCOL

*In which Knut discusses
urgent issues of good order
and mutual respect with
Lion and Sam.*

Knut saw himself saying, largely with gestures: 'Sam; do you wish to remain on the left? You may choose. The choice is yours. You may take the right.'

The dog's place, sir, is the dog's place.

So Sam remained at Knut's left.

'Confirming,' Knut said to Lion, 'that he approves of your position to the right.' Knut indicating the place in mind. 'But at all times, Lion, leave a space. Remember. Remember. Never ahead. Never behind. Or I shall make my presence felt!'

Lion remained out there in his merciful mist of the mind.

Knut trying again with increased authority; without success; but humouring a whimsical idea. Acting the pantomime. Speaking it in Latin of a kind.

Lion, as if settled for ever in his fog, went on licking at his paw while Knut waited a few seconds more.

'Lion,' he said sharply, in an ancient language familiar to his ear, but rarely attempted before. 'To my right. Not ahead or behind. A space between us at all times.'

The mists of the mind – Knut's and Lion's – dispersed with a sigh.

Hebrew, Knut thought. Hebrew, he understands.

The great beast was angling his head as Sam had done, appraising the substance of what he heard. Perhaps weighing the idea of resuming the role of lion instead of playing the phantom which led to so much conjecture. Expanding as if taking in large measures of air. Supporting himself on three feet; curling the fourth against his deep breast. Limping excessively. Considering Knut's instructions. Obeying them after a fashion. Stepping so close that Knut's heartbeat took hold of his throat. Lion settling himself provocatively a hand's breadth from Knut's right knee, ideally placed for dismembering the leg prior to carrying it off for morning tea.

Knut's outrage exploding: *'I said a space to the right! I mean what I say. The three of us in line!'*

Lion glancing along the flank; the possibility of a feline shrug; the likelihood of the comment: 'I see a space.'

Knut roaring with hand and voice in his native tongue: *'Away!'*

Sam poised to flee. Sending distress signals: No, sir. No. Lions can be dragons or gods or any damn' thing. Treat him with respect.

Knut's heart now thudding in his ears. The sword, somewhere behind, was out of reach. Might as well have been out of the world. But there was Lion on Knut's right increasing the gap to ten feet! Perhaps to the inch. Perhaps.

Knut concealing his sigh. 'That's the boy.'

Sam transmitting messages. Wildly. *He's not a boy! NO.*

Knut giving thought to the confusion of voices in his poor

brain. Then taking time out to explain. '*Boy* is a term of convenience, my friends. Reveal yourself to be other than a lion and you'll be addressed accordingly. Sam, if you show yourself to be other than a dog, the same rule will apply. Meanwhile, everyone lives with *boy*! If I can, you can! What's the bind?'

I'm heading, Knut thought, for an identity crisis. I won't know whether I'm bird, beast, demon or cracked. Here's Sam against my leg sending signals like a sinking ship. There's *Panthera leo,* licking at a paw, understanding garbled Hebrew and I couldn't even ask my way to the Wailing Wall!

'Sam! Heel!

'Well done, Lion, but maintain a distance equal to the length of a very long lion or I'll remove you from the planet. Human wit is equal to tooth and claw.'

Dear, dear, said Sam, you'll be the death of us. We'll be flesh and bone and gravy on his dinner plate.

At which point, Knut raised his umbrella, exposing its faces, inner and outer, moving it across his upper body as he would have moved a shield of greater substance.

'My shield, Lion, fences me round with images of wattle gnomes. Their wiles exceed those of taipans and lions. Their power derives from the word-witch who bore me in a brash moment and in whose house I was taught to say as I left for instruction each Sunday:

'*Beware, take care*
of the green-eyed dragon with the thirteen tails;
between thee and me he stands foursquare.'

Knut closed his pronouncement with the clearing of a profoundly husky throat.

THE VOICE CALLS US

*Knut gets closer to discovering
the secret of his father's ziggurat.
He thinks about what it is to be
human and to have no say in
one's own existence. He is left
separate, alone and apart.*

Knut was now stepping out through a wide wheel that held all three abreast until the long, featureless wall on their right ended: the wall that he had first confronted across the square. Fourteen feet high and seven feet thick, matched in parallel by an identical wall a hundred paces distant hard right, thus forming and confining between them a massive, low rectangular building one hundred paces wide and hundreds of paces long.

Knut's stride was now hesitating, was now breaking and stopping. He was confronting, with shock, an amazing departure from the life-style of Richard Canute, architect extraordinary – a highly ornamented façade recessed between the two plain side walls. A façade that formed an immense sculpture of human figures in bas-relief, nude, partially nude, soft, sensitive, tender, filling the frontage from edge to edge, fabricated from or faced with tiles of exquisite shades despite the discolourations of great age. And at its centre, critical to the design, was the profile of a sphere, an unobstructed ring on edge that invited entry. Here it was; the shape of the sphere as remembered by Knut from the plans he had pieced together.

For a time he could not separate his confusions from his opinions and reactions. Could these be the sculptures of the private man, dreamings withheld from his family, never revealed to his contemporaries and opposed to the principles that he championed? Or were they more?

Was I, thought Knut, at best, a boy making an idol of someone like myself? Making a Moses out of ordinary flesh and blood? Did I, did Mother, and did everyone else have eyes only for the mask he wore as he came into the house or went out?

Is it here that Father speaks with his secret voice? The voice he dreamt with? The voice he heard in his sleep? Man on the left in all of his moods deferring to woman in some of her moods, on the right? What happened, really, when they made me that night?

Or do I, thought Knut, see images of what it is to be human and to have no say in it? To be born as one finds oneself. To be separate, alone and apart. To be left to grow into one or the other as best as one can. Into the woman or the man for the new survival and the new start. Or is it an image of Father's youth and manhood, his prime and decline? Is it the rise and fall of every human, woman or man?

When this work was planned, he must have been convinced I was dead. He would know I would never have run away, leaving life behind, running out. But I must not credit him with more than he has said.

What I see, architecturally, are images of my love and of me. If all the world that used to be could stand where I stand now, might each person say the same? 'These sculptures are of my love and of me.'

My partners, thought Knut! Have they run? Have they abandoned me?

No.

Sam was at heel. Lion was a dozen long, strong strides behind, looking some other way. The classical figure. The lion chiselled from stone.

With gentleness, Knut said, 'Come along, my friend. Please.'

Lion, with the curve of his back, expressing the great burden of the wounds to his flesh and spirit.

'We take care of one another,' Knut said. 'The rules may be old. May be allegorical. May be much abused. But here they will be honoured.'

Lion could have said: Am I a dog, a demon, a dragon? What am I but the King of Beasts who must keep his place or suffer the consequences?

'Humans like me,' Knut said, 'were taught – were indoctrinated, perhaps – that the world was made for them and all other creatures were in their custody and care. How much of that world remains, or how little, who knows? And who am I to say how little or how much of the decree was imaginary, impractical or ignored? But I was raised to live by it. With one exclusion insisted upon by Father. I was never to regard myself as the sacrificial lamb to speed the ambitions of another. I do not require it of you either. You're my lion and my sword. I'm your human and your shield.'

Sam said: Which makes what of me?

'Most likely the only male specimen of your kind. But you are as God fashioned you in the wild. If He has brought you this far, would He have left you alone? Are you not like me? No threat to any friendly creature? But pity the creature, I say, that starts in against you or me.'

Knut was perplexed by his reply. And turned away. And made a study of standing. And Sam adjusted his position at the left and Lion closed in to three paces.

'Thank you,' Knut said, and shortly, as if mildly enchanted, he approached the outer threshold of the central ring; that profile of a sphere. The ring itself was wide enough to admit all three in a stretched line abreast. Wide enough and wide open, though it offered no view of what lay within. As if indeed a mist was within; or nothing was there. Knut then came to understand that dog and lion were settling, were sitting, were bristling, perhaps from sensitivity to alarms or deterrents of which he, as a human, had no perception.

Yes, Knut thought. Yes. But what does this mean?

In my case, perhaps, I may be able to pass directly through. If I'm the right one, it's unlikely that entry will be refused. If I'm the wrong one, wouldn't I have perished before now? But how am I to go on in without my friends? I have given my bond. They, too, must be the ones or they wouldn't be here and wouldn't have tested me at such strenuous risk to themselves.

I note the absence of the voices that came with me into this new world. I hear nothing from anywhere now. All predictions, warnings, illuminations, encouragements and feelings have ceased. Everything is silent except for the conviction that I must go on in.

Knut said to his friends, 'It's not your time. It's mine. Wait until nightfall, then seek a safe place. Wait again tomorrow. And the day after. And the day after that. Go on waiting until I call. Then come at once and swiftly.'

Knut stripped himself of everything that he wore and of everything that he carried.

All these items that he removed from himself he placed at his feet and, naked, stepped over them and walked on and through the ring. When he looked back, seeking Sam and Lion, there was nothing to see but mist or vacuum.

For a time, breath was not easy to draw and Knut's tremblings were too great to suppress. His vision was poor; but in the light, here, inside the threshold formed by the ring, a spacious walkway began. Wide and high and long. As wide as it was high and becoming a deeper and deeper gloom in its distance directly ahead.

What I see here, Knut thought, has nothing to do with any plans I might ever have pieced together. This conception must come from a later date; from an exercise that came to be championed by influential people; even by heads of governments and nations resolving to make a human statement in terrible days of worsening trouble.

Why am I, Knut Mannerheim Canute, at its centre? Father was the architect. Yes. Someone had to be.

I was nothing but a kid who went missing; who vanished. How could I ever have been more? Except for that one strange night when Aunt Ingrid and I made an audience of two for a famous man, Phillip Hann, who travelled from England to be there. Who showed me a fire-lighter of extraordinary design. The same fire-lighter that I found on the rough-hewn table at the edge of the piazza way back there at the top of the stairs. The same fire-lighter that I would not touch, that I left behind.

At which point, Knut paused, and stopped, and went down on his knees.

'Sire,' he said, his voice barely audible, 'as unworthy as I am, it must be so. You must have brought me here. I must confess it and profess it. Your hand must be upon me.'

A soft sound, a slow rhythm, sixty beats to the minute, began to reach Knut on his knees and touch him, and to lift him, as if it derived from the corner of Sebastian and Johann Streets where Bach for breakfast went with high days, holidays and weekends.

Knut stood erect, breathless and shivering, and allowed himself to be drawn into the walkway and to be provoked to an almost feminine lifting of his hands. He was hearing oboe, strings, adult male voices and the Boys' Choir of Tolzer, Austria.

'From this sacred sound,' Father said long, long, long ago, 'renew yourself when you are perplexed, when you are confused, when life has more to say than you understand. For me, in all of space and time, there cannot be a purer sound. Hail Johann Sebastian Bach. And I've heard people ask why on Earth did we buy such a house on streets so strangely named.'

Knut moving to the sound, compulsively, step by step, second by second. Slower by far than the beating of his heart. As sung in Vienna when he was just born. *Sleepers awake. The Voice calls us.* It was calling Knut now, on an unnamed date of an unnamed century, wrapping its rhythm and its sound all around, ahead, within, and behind.

On either side of this walkway, under glass, Knut became aware of major works of art; of the epic and the tragedy of the human adventure; of mosaics, frescoes and statuary created by the masters, even by the ancients. A gallery arched through its length, with a clear substance above, reinforced, ribbed, but admitting little light. Heaped externally with debris, with the spoil of centuries, except at its apex which gave entry to stray rays of light. Making the way beautiful. Making it dreadful.

Knut was barely able to ask: 'How can it be?'

But he heard his own voice replying: 'We've destroyed ourselves because we were free. We've despoiled the forests. We've melted the icecaps. We've flooded the seas, the plains and the hills. We left billions to perish in suffocating mud or in poisoned mountain air. Upon the peak of one such mountain this ziggurat was formed and here it stands. God only knows what agonies it must have seen.'

At four hundred and thirty beats, four hundred and thirty seconds, the rhythm had gone. No longer were the voices calling. No more was there anyone to awake.

Knut stood naked, shivering, losing strength, knowing that the gallery had come to a dim and darkened end, a rear wall of unadorned mud brick around fourteen feet high and seven feet thick. Matching the walls as seen outside.

Knut leant there, mourning the death and the ending of all that he had known.

'My darling, my darling, my darling Nanette . . .'

There Knut slid down the wall. There he huddled at its base. There he was overcome by a sleep of unimaginable exhaustion, tormented by sounds or dreams of roaring, everlasting rain.

PART FIVE
THE JOURNEY
ENDS AND
BEGINS

NO DOOR BUT ONE

*Knut is confronted with
choices: 'I will serve You only
while You allow me to express
a point of view.' He becomes
a man . . .*

Knut awoke at the foot of the wall to a warming shaft of sunlight that forced him to move back into shadow, almost into
dark. And, at a disturbing distance, defined by afternoon light,
he saw the ring through which he had entered, no detail visible
in the glare beyond.

He filled his lungs and cried: *'Sam! Lion! Come! Come!
Come!'*

His voice broke and he feared it would be lost until
shockingly it crashed and rang and echoed in his ears.

Knut waited for Sam and Lion, while his fright and anguish
underwent change, while they became a memory; a mere irrita-
tion. But Sam and Lion showed no inclination that they wished
to pass through the ring. And no inclination to come through to
be with him? Which, Knut believed, implied the pressure or
influence of an outside source.

He demanded: 'I require them to come. The right to enter the ziggurat is theirs just as it was mine. It's a right they have not assumed. It's a right they have won.'

Knut waited.

Then stating: 'If You're the God we've been told about, if You're the God I believe in, you must know that I love them. Let them come.'

Knut went on waiting.

Then declared: 'If love doesn't move God, I'll have none of Him.'

Knut striding off through the gallery. Back through the chasms of gloom and the beams of sunlight. Ignoring the silent works of the Masters. Discounting, dismissing and disclaiming the compulsion that had driven him to march through them.

'If Sam and Lion don't come,' he cried, 'I will march straight on and out and never enter again!'

Knut's friends came into view, hastening.

Knut, with his left arm about Sam and his right hand on Lion, said: 'Sire, you know I'm my father's son. Why drive me to distraction by testing me again and again?'

In the way unique to the dog, Sam said: 'I led the way. I came first.'

And in the way of Lion, Lion said: 'I came second. But I came.'

To which in English, Knut replied: 'Together you waited through whatever the weather has done and in common we are one. And together we will do what I elect to do when I know the choices that I have.'

Immediately, the possibility of choices began to appear.

Earlier, Knut might have given thought to the idea of doors;

logically seven, for in matters of the kind the sacred number of seven was the rule. But he saw only three. Three doors, the possibility of three choices; not seven. Knut could have been aware of them before – as panels celebrating the beauty of cedar, oak, and pine.

Each door was of uncommon width and height and uniformly banded with bronze. All were without obvious means of exit or entry. No knobs to turn. No latches. No keyholes. But doors they were, beyond a doubt, and of great interest, for they stood at the point of his reunion with Lion and Sam.

Knut was dwelling on that observation while the light rapidly continued to fade.

'Thank You,' Knut said, 'for putting my fellow creatures on hold. For bringing them to me. But they're temporal, as am I. I know that each door may well conceal the future. I know that each will lead to a future that will come to an end as all futures must. But I will not choose from doors that stay closed. I will not choose from any door that I cannot see.

'Far, far behind me in time, I was conceived on a mountain. For You, Sire, that may have been but a moment ago; but I am aware that You may feel everyone's moment, moment by moment, however extraordinary or incomprehensible that it seems. Yet by Your intervention I have suffered all the agonies of the born, all the agonies of the dying and many of the agonies of the dead. Is this a fair game?

'You plucked me from my world and separated me from those I love. You threw me into the ether and put me down in Your Own Good Time. What's done is done. Who am I to dispute what You have done? But what comes next will be chosen by *me*!'

Later, Knut said, 'I derive from a family of kings, convicts and mountaineers and will serve You only while You allow me to express a point of view. My name, I dare to know, is Adam; but I ask, what has happened to Eve? Why are we not together, hand in hand, as once we were when I was seventeen? I wait on the answer.'

All light had gone and within the focus of the great ziggurat darkness was complete and Sam was under Adam's left hand and Lion was under his right. Each immediate and warm.

Through the left hand, a voice said, *Sir; wherever you go I will guard Adam's door.*

Through the right hand, a different voice said, *I will defend Adam at his command. He is my shield, but I am his sword.*

Within this dark and silent place a pale rectangle began to assume the shape of an area of light; a tall window or partly opened door, inviting Adam's inspection of a greyed skyline of broken rooftops, blasted windowpanes, chimneystacks falling down, disintegrating steeples and an appalling, continuing rain.

Adam drew closer, and believed himself to be on an upper floor of what might once have been a residential building with expansive and expensive city views. At the point of stepping through onto a narrow balcony, he drew back. He declined.

'You're not playing the game,' Adam said. 'I knew You wouldn't.'

No reprimand came, but the voice of the prophet said: 'This is the house that Mankind prepared for you. Take it and make of it what you will.'

'I'll make nothing of it,' Adam said. 'I'm alone and on my

own. I do as I say. Let it fall. Who'd want it? Am I an army of a million men? Am I like Him with a few billion hands?'

A pressure started bearing against Adam's heart from within and he searched in the dark for his Lion and his Sam.

He called them, but they did not, or would not, or could not come.

CHAPTER
FORTY-FIVE

THE ENDLESS
PRESENCE

*Gone are the long, dark
centuries.*

Around Adam a light grew of a different hue – rosy red, spreading from a rectangle on its broad edge, in the shape of a window with curtains parted just a little. A great city was at rest beyond and a clock with small red numerals read 1.17 a.m.

'Oh, God,' Adam cried, 'what are You up to now? You wouldn't, You couldn't be so unkind! Where, in such a place, would I find my love?'

The voice of endless compassion said: 'Those you love, my son, have ministered unto you through these long, dark centuries, but I am the one whose love came first. I made you as you are and you made me as I am. I nourished you before you uttered my name. Open wide the curtains, my honey-bunny, we're almost home.'

'I can't go back!' Adam cried. 'I am what I am what I am. I'm not what I was any more. There's nowhere to go but here.'

Long afterwards, he felt about in the dark for his Lion and his Sam and crawled different ways. Many times he called, and often he crawled, but he remained alone.

...

Adam opened his eyes at last, at last, upon a great space, a boundless presence of soft light; it was a dawn or an evening in an unblemished garden ready to be made into a world of his own inclination.

But Adam saw it in fright and shock, distressed almost out of his mind, crying wildly as if tearing apart, clasping at agonies along his lengths and depths and within his heart. Shrieking: *'Sam! Lion! Sam! Lion! Come! Come!'*

They were there – and his agonies passed and his breathing became quiet, until, in a monumental moment of understanding, he saw at his side, in reach of his marvelling, tentative touch, the only one he ever had loved in that way. Born again from within himself, the young woman Nanette, Eve.

He had carried her like a jewel in his heart for a thousand years.

She stirred and smiled and laughed and cried.

'You've grown a beard, my darling! You've got a *beard*, my darling! Oh, my love.'

The voice of the Eternal was heard in the land: 'Be fruitful. Multiply.'

ABOUT THE AUTHOR

Ivan Southall, born in 1921, grew up in Surrey Hills, Victoria, Australia. His first story was published in the Melbourne *Herald* when he was twelve years old.

The death of his father ended his schooling and at age fourteen he started work, eventually becoming a copy boy at the *Herald*. There he hoped to become a reporter, but was apprenticed to the Pictorial Department instead. He went on writing in his spare time and finished four books before he turned twenty. Much revised and developed, all were published later, one as recently as 1983.

During the Second World War, Ivan Southall became captain of a Sunderland flying boat and was awarded the Distinguished Flying Cross. Afterwards, he wrote war history at the R.A.A.F. Headquarters in London.

Back in Australia, Ivan began a full-time writing career and many books now bear his name. His work has been published in over twenty languages: *Ash Road*, *To the Wild Sky*, *Bread and Honey* and *Fly West* each became an Australian Children's Book of the Year. *Sly Old Wardrobe*, with drawings by Ted Greenwood, was Australian Picture Book of the Year, and the novel *Josh* won the British Carnegie Medal. *The Long Night Watch* received in Australia the inaugural National Children's Book Award. Japan, Holland, Austria, the United States, Spain and the IBBY awards (International Board on Books for Young People) have also honoured his work.

Ivan Southall has lectured widely in Australia and abroad. In 1973 he delivered the Whittall Poetry and Literature Lecture at the

Library of Congress, and in 1974 he gave the Arbuthnot Honor Lecture for the American Library Association at the University of Washington. *A Journey of Discovery* reprints some of these lectures.

In 1981, Ivan was appointed to the Order of Australia and in 1993 received an Emeritus Award from the Australia Council for his contribution to literature. His home is in the foothills of the Victorian Alps, where he grows produce for home use and, for ten years, has been developing new fuchsias. To date, seventy-five of these have been registered internationally.

His Californian-born wife, Susan, is an artist; she grows roses, has bred Japanese Spitz dogs and has written two books for children.

Ivan, with ten grandchildren and two great-grandchildren, has one son and three daughters by his former marriage to Joy. Andrew is an artist, Roberta runs a plant nursery, Elizabeth is an editor, and Melissa, who is handicapped, lives in a pleasant community not far from the sea.

Ivan worked for nearly five years on *Ziggurat*, his most astoundingly innovative book for young adult readers.